Twayne's United States Authors Series

Sylvia E. Bowman, *Editor*

INDIANA UNIVERSITY

John Muir

JOHN MUIR

by **HERBERT F. SMITH**
University of Wisconsin

 73

Twayne Publishers, Inc.　　::　　New York

MANUFACTURED IN THE UNITED STATES OF AMERICA BY
UNITED PRINTING SERVICES, INC.
NEW HAVEN, CONN.

For v.m.s.

Preface

WRITING about the works of John Muir as literature is a little like attempting a critical summary of the Paul Bunyan legends, or attempting to analyze stylistically the writings of Abraham Lincoln. Muir exists primarily as a person, and it is as a folk hero, as a historic figure, as a remarkable manifestation of one element of what we like to consider as the American character that he has been studied. All the studies of Muir have been perceptive and telling in their relation of Muir as a man; none has adequately shown how he managed to achieve *literature* —ten volumes of it, in the Sierra Edition—out of the most unlikely material. And it is, after all, this capacity which Muir had to write beautifully about wild nature which led to his other successes as a man—his work for conservation, his defense of the American wilderness, his heroic stature in today's America of television watchers.

The paradox of Muir's modern fame is that his works are largely unread, while his name lives on, not only in place-names like Muir Glacier, Muir Woods, and Muir Knoll, but in the American imagination at large. During the time I was working on Muir, I encountered few Americans who had not heard of him and knew something of his mountaineering exploits, fewer still, alas, who had ever read anything by him. Surely the Zen beatniks who roam the Sierras and find in high and lonely places the same sublimity that Muir felt there ought to read his works; yet it is doubtful that they do. Their own writing would profit from the acquaintance. Naturalists, ecologists, botanists, geologists read Muir, but are likely merely to consider him as "quaint" and as a popularizer of science. They may take issue with him over certain details of his scientific observation, but they rarely see his writings in the perspective of their literary qualities.

This study, although it necessarily deals in part with Muir's life—for all of Muir's writings were to some extent autobiographical—is entirely devoted to a close examination of the texts of Muir's works. Any biographical information included beyond the bare facts of Muir's life is intended to throw light on the texts, not on the man. I had no intention to compete with Linnie Marsh Wolfe's *John Muir: Son of the Wilderness* (New York: Knopf, 1945) in laying bare the events of a truly remarkable life. Nor, beyond what are acceptable minimum limits, I hope, have I attempted any analysis of Muir's contribution to science. I have no qualifications whatsoever as a naturalist except those available to anyone who scraped through a year of geology in college and who loves the outdoors.

What I have tried to do in this study is to isolate the literary qualities of Muir's writing from the merely factual and informative, to deduce his metaphysics on the one hand and to examine and analyze the style of his writing on the other. My conclusions as to the extent of Muir's idealism and the subtlety of his writing may thus be verified by the reader at any and all points. For this reason, I have chosen to examine only easily available texts of Muir's work, and have quoted these works liberally. I have followed the chronology of Muir's life, in general, as it is revealed in his autobiographical writings, except for certain details in chapter four which spanned too many years. Chapter six is a summary of Muir's place in American literature with evidence drawn from all periods of his life.

I wish to thank the Wisconsin Alumni Research Foundation for its assistance in the pursuance of this subject; Professor Hugh Iltis, curator of the botanical collection at the University of Wisconsin, for his help in the verification of certain technical points; and Miss Sylvia Bowman for her editorial assistance.

HERBERT F. SMITH

University of Wisconsin

Acknowledgments

I am grateful to the following for permissions to quote material from the works listed:

Russell & Russell, Inc., New York, for material from *Nature in American Literature* by Norman Foerster.

Houghton Mifflin Company, Boston, for selections used from *John of the Mountains, Story of My Boyhood and Youth, A Thousand Mile Walk, My First Summer in the Sierra, Travels in Alaska, Our National Parks, The Mountains of California, The Cruise of the Corwin, Steep Trails,* and *Life and Letters,* all by John Muir.

Mrs. Jean Hanna Clark, for material—poetry and prose—quoted from a letter of Muir to the Pelton family.

Contents

Chronology

1838   April 21, John Muir born in Dunbar, Scotland, son of Daniel Muir and Ann Gilrye Muir.

1849   February 19, the Muir family sailed from Glasgow, Scotland, to New York; the family then moved to a homestead in Buffalo Township, near Portage, Wisconsin.

1860   September, John Muir left home to exhibit his inventions at the Wisconsin State Agricultural Fair in Madison.

1861   January, enrolled at University of Wisconsin.

1863   Left University of Wisconsin intending to attend medical school at the University of Michigan.

1864-   Odd jobs in Canada; inventor in a broom factory; offered
1867   a partnership in Osgood, Smith & Co., carriage manufacturers in Indianapolis; nearly lost sight in an accident; decided to tramp the wilderness as a vocation.

1867   September 2 to January, 1868, walking tour from Indianapolis to Florida and then went to Cuba.

1868   March 28, arrived in San Francisco. Worked on a sheep ranch in lowlands.

1869   Spent "first summer in the Sierra" helping to herd sheep.

1870   In the Yosemite with LeConte geological expedition.

1871   Visit of Emerson with Muir in Yosemite.

1871-   Development of his glacial theory of the origin of Yosemite;
1875   controversy with Josiah D. Whitney.

1879   First Alaska trip, with S. Hall Young.

1880   Married Louie Wanda Strentzel, April 14. Second Alaska trip, July-September.

1881   Third Alaska trip, aboard the *Corwin*.

1890   Yosemite National Park Bill passed, largely as a result of Muir's two articles in *Century Magazine*.

1893-   Visited Europe. Published *The Mountains of California*.
1894

1899   Member of the Harriman-Alaska Expedition.

1901   Published *Our National Parks*.

1905   Yosemite Valley receded to United State National Park Service. Death of Louie Strentzel Muir, August 6.

1909   Published *Stickeen*.

1911   Published *My First Summer in the Sierra*.

1912   Published *The Yosemite*.

1913   Published *The Story of My Boyhood and Youth*.

1914   Died, Los Angeles, December 24.

1915-   *The Sierra Edition of the Works of John Muir*, William F.
1924   Badé, editor.

1938   *John of the Mountains*, Muir's journals published; Linnie Marsh Wolfe, editor.

Neither let it be deemed too sawcie a comparison to ballance the highest poynt of man's wit with the efficacie of Nature, but rather give right honor to the heavenly Maker of that maker.

—Sidney, *Apologie for Poetrie*

CHAPTER 1

A Different Drummer

PROBABLY the most persistent cliché of criticism of American Transcendentalist writers is that they found written expression difficult, that they were more at home writing in their journals than when writing for publication. Most of Emerson's essays are essentially lectures; Thoreau's output of works published in his lifetime is meager compared to his voluminous journals; and John Muir did not write his first book until he was fifty-six years old. These men, the cliché continues, were more interested in living their lives than in writing about them. Emerson was "the great example." Thoreau's "profession was living." Muir was "a supersalesman of nature."[1]

All of these statements carry the implication that writing was for Emerson, Thoreau, and Muir an occasional pursuit carried on in their spare time, that they felt somehow writing lacked the dignity of great thoughts or great actions. The misconception, as it relates to John Muir, is the harder to eradicate because there is some truth in it. Muir did say that he "would rather stand in what all the world would call an idle manner, literally gaping with all the mouths of soul and body" than to narrow his "attention to bookmaking."[2] But the conceptions of writers about themselves are not always to be believed. The existence of a journal which is more than a simple diary may be taken, I believe, as *prima facie* evidence that the author hopes and intends to become a writer. Muir left behind him sixty volumes of journals.

Furthermore, though Muir did not publish his first book until his fifty-sixth year, he had been writing for periodicals since he was thirty-three. Though his literary output during his youth and middle age was quite limited, he spent many years polishing, in his notebooks and in his periodical publications, a fluent style. Still, he was too busy during most of his first years in California to write much unless he had a pressing purpose. Vistas of mountains and unexplored regions stretched before him during his prime years; and, committed to a life in nature compared to which Thoreau's was that of a suburban commuter, Muir had endlessly that one more peak to climb before setting to the hard work of converting his experience to literature. His life was so full that it is a wonder that he had time to keep his sixty journals, let alone revise any of them for publication. But he did, and in the volumes which represent his life work, he stands forth as much the man of letters as the man of action.

This study takes as a starting point the assumption that Muir was in all of his writings a conscious artist. Though I will examine some of the ancillary values of various writings of his— the scientific value of his glaciation studies and the guide-book and travelogue value of others—my primary interest will be in Muir's writings as belles-lettres. They constitute, I believe, a remarkable postscript to the great Transcendental productions of Emerson and Thoreau; and, though they begin with a received version of Romantic philosophy, they become in time purely Muir's own in their concepts and criticisms of nature, civilization, and other aspects of life upon which Muir commented often wisely and invariably well.

His life divides into periods which are reflected by his work. His boyhood and youth, a period of seedtime and prospects in which he suggests the first indications of his choice of nature against civilization, are reflected in *The Story of My Boyhood and Youth* (1913). The first fruits of that decision to "consider the lilies, how they grow," were related in a journal kept of *A Thousand Mile Walk to the Gulf* (1916), one of the posthumous works edited from his journals. In it one can observe the case history of Muir's mind recording, as the events take place, the gradual clearing away of doubt about the wisdom of a decision made. *A Thousand Mile Walk,* perhaps the most revealing of Muir's works and certainly one dealing with the most crucial period of his life, is a classic of Transcendental introspection as well as of natural observation.

The crucial decision made, little was left for Muir to do but discover California, or, more particularly, the Sierra, where his peculiar talents and purposes could find a fitting surrounding. The period of exploration, of observation, of natural and scientific analysis, and of discovery lasted some twenty years, little enough time when one considers the vast spaces involved. This period is bountifully recorded in several kinds of publications, making it beneficial to the reader interested in the varieties of Muir's experience. Immediate perceptions and revelations are given in Mrs. Wolfe's edition of Muir's journals, *John of the Mountains* (1938). More ordered description, less subjectively interpreted, is available to the reader who cares to search out Muir's contributions from 1875 to 1900 in *Century Magazine*, in *Harper's Magazine*, and in *The Atlantic Monthly*. Muir's more considered revisions of this data are given final form in *My First Summer in the Sierra* (1911) and in *The Mountains of California* (1894). Other ephemera of the period were collected by William F. Badé in *Steep Trails*, Volume VIII of the Sierra Edition.

A fourth period is rather hard to separate from the third. All the time Muir was exploring the Sierras and recording his impressions and observations of nature and man, another intense interest was taking shape and moving toward the need for action—the problem of conservation. Much of Muir's writings about his explorations were intended to urge conservation, but his more direct work toward saving national forests and parks came after his earlier, more exuberant period. *Our National Parks* (1901) and *The Yosemite* (1912) best represent this period in his life.

The final period of Muir's life is a conglomeration, but amazing biographically because he retained such vigor at an age when most men are, at best, writing their memoirs. Trips to Europe, to 'South America and Africa, and explorations among the glaciers of the coast of Alaska mark this period. The Alaska phase is represented in his writing by *Stickeen* (1909), *The Cruise of the Corwin* (1918) and *Travels in Alaska* (1915), while for the foreign explorations and Muir's situation late in life, one must read (sometimes between the lines) his *Life and Letters*, by William Frederick Badé (1924) and the journals edited by Mrs. Wolfe.[3]

I   *Emotion Recollected in Tranquillity*

Most of Muir's writings have about them a sensation of hardship overcome. Whether edited by Muir himself or posthumously by his editors, the works that have found publication between hard covers mostly stem from journals and notes kept on odd pieces of paper, some of them "scribbled by flickering campfires when his body was numb with fatigue; or in the dark lee of some boulder or tree while the storm raged without; or tramping over a vast glacier, his fingers stiff with cold, and his eyes blinded by the snow glare" (*John of the Mountains*, xv). *The Story of My Boyhood and Youth* is an exception. In its original form, it was dictated at the estate of Edward H. Harriman on Klamath Lake, Oregon, to Harriman's own personal secretary, who followed Muir everywhere he went during a vacation, taking down his every word. The result, well over one thousand pages of typescript, was then edited by Muir to its present size.[4]

The unusual nature of this process of composition accounts for several peculiarities of the book. It has many ellipses. Some are adducible to faulty memory; the events covered in the book were fifty to sixty years old to Muir when he dictated them. Other ellipses are undoubtedly a result of the painful nature of Muir's memories. His relationship with his father, in particular, was such that he could not tell all his feelings, even though his father had been dead for thirty-three years when he wrote *The Story of My Boyhood and Youth*.

Another peculiarity of the book, but a charming one, is its conversational tone. Organized in a roughly chronological form from John's youth in Dunbar, Scotland, to his young manhood in Wisconsin and his brief college experience at the University of Wisconsin, it is full of digressions apparently caused by the free-associative flow of memories. What the narrative loses in orderly arrangement because of these digressions it more than makes up for by the pleasure of the anecdotes recorded and by the insight granted into the workings of John Muir's mind. Thus, the chapter entitled "A New World" purports to describe Muir's sensations upon his arrival in Wisconsin, but it actually skips back and forth between the old and new worlds as memories of first views of American birds and flowers prompt earlier recollections of similar, and at times quite dissimilar, old world birds and anecdotes about them. No man ever believed more completely than John Muir that "a touch of nature makes the whole world kin,"[5] and his delight in the similarities of wild nature in America and Europe becomes, in the light of his total work, a revealing glimpse into his ideas about nature.

But one perhaps should not read *Boyhood and Youth* in the way one reads Muir's other writings more specifically dedicated to natural description. Although all of his work is autobiographical in the sense that his observations and travels seem to be the center of the work, this book has as its real protagonist John

Muir and not nature itself. The central conflict in nearly all of his writing is the opposition of nature and culture. In *Boyhood and Youth* particularly, but somewhat less in the next two books to be considered, this opposition of nature and culture takes the form of a spiritual struggle in Muir himself. The symbols of opposition are set very clearly in this volume; they are the boy, John Muir, and his father, Daniel Muir. *The Story of My Boyhood and Youth* is, at its foundation, the story of a struggle between opposite creeds and opposed generations.

II *Father and Son*

John Muir goes into very few details about the conditioning process that made Daniel Muir a harsh tyrant as a father. Having come to revere his father as father, he accepted, in *Boyhood and Youth,* the fact of Daniel Muir's severe fundamentalist religion and felt it necessary only to show the means and results of his own reaction to it. Daniel Muir was orphaned soon after he was born (1804) into the most brutal poverty. His early years were a constant struggle for survival, in which he succeeded, finally, in ameliorating his circumstances. By means of two successful marriages he had become, when John was born, a fairly successful middle-class merchant in Dunbar, Scotland. Unfortunately for his family, the one characteristic of his poverty which he carried into his new condition in life was a peculiarly harsh opiate of hell-fire breathing fundamentalism. He had been converted at an early age to an extreme sect of Presbyterianism, and much of his later life was spent trying to achieve again the ecstasy of wild emotion of that experience. He was not constant to any one creed throughout his life and never settled into a routine of worship. Whatever new form of belief came along, as long as it was more extreme than the one he practiced presently, was likely to bring him in as a convert.

Perhaps he knew that his own pleasure in his religion was at least partly a result of his freedom to choose whatever manifestation of spirit would give him greatest pleasure; but this knowledge had no influence upon his treatment of his family. John's mother, Ann Gilrye Muir, seems to have succumbed more to the charms of Daniel's beliefs than to his personality when she married him, and possibly he took her action as evidence of their power. Or, more likely, he merely exercised the rights which both Scotch custom and law gave to the head of a family in the matter of religious persuasion. At any rate, his control over the devotions of his family was total. There was one God in the Muir household, and Daniel was his prophet. For Daniel, He was a God of wrath who found evil in the most casual acts of childish insouciance. And He authorized Daniel to punish these acts with the greatest severity whenever they occurred.

John Muir makes the best case possible for his father in *Boyhood and Youth*. Many incidents are recorded in which Daniel appears as the patient father preparing his children for life. To encourage their husbandry, for example, he gave each child a corner of the garden of the house in Dunbar to do with as he wished. "We planted what we liked best," Muir recorded, "wondering how the hard dry seeds could change into soft leaves and flowers and find their way out to the light" (*Boyhood and Youth*, 11). Daniel also gave his sons good advice when the time came for them to learn how to swim. "Go to the frogs," he said, "and they will give you all the lessons you need" (101). The technique worked. At first the boys found it hard to imitate "the smooth, comfortable sliding gait of our amphibious teachers," but eventually they found themselves "about as amphibious as frogs" (102).

Such examples of sympathy between the generations are rare in Muir's account of his boyhood. More often Daniel Muir was the harsh taskmaster, physical and moral, who believed that sweat and pain were the only means to achieve heaven, that the acts of childhood and love of nature were synonymous with evil, and that both represented dangerous tendencies to be whipped out of a boy. Muir did his best to defend or excuse his father. He equated the frequent whippings with Scottish harshness in general and admitted their pragmatic value. He noticed that certain of the lessons of the lash remained, "that there was a close connection between the skin and the memory, and that irritating the skin excited the memory to any required degree" (28). But he gave away his true feelings about his father almost accidentally. Incidents of his youth which had the greatest influence upon him he describes in the most dispassionate tone, but the intensity of the writing reveals the depths of his feelings.

The best example in *The Story of My Boyhood and Youth* of such a deep psychic wound suffered at the hands of his father is the story of how John dug the family well for their second farm, "Hickory Hill." The well had to be ninety feet deep, eighty feet through a fine, hard sandstone. John was given the

task alone, and " had to sit cramped in a space about three feet
in diameter, and wearily chip, chip, with heavy hammer and
chisels from early morning until dark, day after day, for weeks
and months" (184). Death almost relieved him of his task
when through ignorance, Daniel Muir almost allowed him to
become asphyxiated from the effects of carbonic acid gas. But
after John had recuperated in "a day or two," his father sent
him down into the well again to finish the project. Muir's
account of the incident is recorded objectively, except for one
metaphoric parallel which he allowed himself at the end of the
account: "Constant dropping wears away stone. So does constant
chipping, while at the same time wearing away the chipper.
Father never spent an hour in that well" (186). The comment
reveals, as much by what it does *not* say as by what it says, the
intensity of his feelings about his father.

Most of the differences between the two generations recorded
by Muir in this book are of the classic pattern of "Fathers and
Sons." The natural wildness of youth and the thoughtlessness that
goes with it were incomprehensible to Daniel Muir. He forbade
his sons to roam the fields near Dunbar on Saturdays, restricting
them to the closed, however spacious, backyard of their home.
The boys, "like devout martyrs of wildness," stole away at
every opportunity anyway, then compounded their felony by
having too poor a sense of time to return before nightfall (37).
The fact that their disobedience was innocent provided no
excuse. Fighting was just as sure a means of getting a "skelping"
—two in fact, one from the parent and another from the teacher.
But neither John nor any other boy could resist the temptation,
and Daniel Muir was not one to see that his deterrent did
not deter.

Along with the classic symptoms of the war of the generations
are evidences in *The Story of My Boyhood and Youth* of the
unusual rebellion of John Muir. The extremity of his father's
harshness and of John's own peculiar genius made the difficulties
in the Muir household radical, both in their appearance and in
their resolution. John defeated his father at every turn, out-
witting him in the matter of liberties and by outstudying him on
Daniel's own strongest point, the knowledge of the Bible, to the
point where John could quote more texts in favor of an action
than Daniel could cite against it. When Daniel Muir took up
vegetarianism, it was John who convinced him that he was in

error by quoting the example of Elijah, who was fed flesh by the ravens at the command of God.

Daniel objected to John's scientific study. "The Bible," he ordered, "is the only book human beings can possibly require throughout all the journey from earth to heaven." But his son pointed out that Daniel himself could not read his Bible without the aid of spectacles; the science of optics was justified therefore by Daniel's own rule. Daniel had to agree, but he did so with bad grace, cursing his son as "a contumacious quibbler too fond of disputation" (194). In a way, one can hardly refuse sympathy to poor beleaguered Daniel Muir (if he had not abused his right to corporal punishment); his know-it-all son would have tried the patience of a saint!

John also played, katzenjammer-kid fashion, on one of Daniel Muir's strongest virtues—his willingness to keep his word. When his father objected to John's reading at odd times during the day, John asked and received permission to get up early in the morning to read. He then began to arise at one o'clock in the morning, glorying in the prospect of having acquired five hours to himself. When his father reprimanded him for waking so early, John reminded him that he had given his permission. " 'I *know* it,' he said, in an almost agonized tone of voice, 'I *know* I gave you that miserable permission, but I never imagined that you would get up in the middle of the night' " (200).

Thus did John Muir act out his own life's example of an archetypal struggle. It was at least partly a reaction to the harsh God of Daniel Muir that made John Muir wish to escape from civilized creeds to the softer sanctity of wild nature. In *Boyhood and Youth* the theme of his father's influence upon him and his reaction to that influence is a striking symbol of the central theme of the book, the opposition of civilization and wild nature. Though the most obvious, it is only one way in which Muir shows the conflict between these two opposites. Much more attention is given in the book to John Muir's own dawning ideas about life, about the relative merits of tameness, of acceptance of received opinions, and of wildness and independence.

III *Nature and Revelation*

The reader of *The Story of My Boyhood and Youth* ought to remember the fact that the book was dictated fifty years after most of the events described in it. Muir ascribes, in retrospect, a great deal of importance to his wild Saturday excursions, purchased at the cost of near-certain whippings, to bird fields and meadows in Scotland. "Wildness was ever sounding in our ears," he wrote. "Nature saw to it that besides school lessons and church lessons some of her own lessons should be learned, perhaps with a view to the time when we should be called to wander in wildness to our heart's content" (41). The use of the first person plural is editorial. "We," the mass of middle-class children growing up in Scotland of the 1840's and in Wisconsin of the 1850's, did not free themselves from the burden of civilization and revealed religion. Only John Muir did. *The Story of My Boyhood and Youth* explains how the process began.

The description, except insofar as it relates to John's opposition to his father, is rarely overt. Muir's technique instead is to juxtapose two scenes, one of nature wild, the other of a contrasting and debased tameness. It is a remarkable technique, subtly and poetically used. Though examples of the technique may be found throughout the work, there is none better than his description of the boys' feelings about the skylarks of Scotland. The narrative begins with a description of one of the boys' games, a contest between them to observe a lark in its flight for the longest time: "And finally only one of us would be left to claim that he still saw him. At last he, too, would have to admit that the singer had soared beyond his sight, and still the music came pouring down to us in glorious profusion, from a height far above our vision, requiring marvelous power of voice, for that rich, delicious, soft, and yet clear music was distinctly heard long after the bird was out of sight. Then, suddenly ceasing, the glorious singer would appear, falling like a bolt straight down to his nest where his mate was sitting on the eggs" (39).

Immediately following this lyric description is a discussion of how the boys would cage young larks, sometimes succeeding "in keeping one alive for a year or two." Muir carefully described a process which must have seemed peculiarly inhuman to him: how the boys carefully placed sods from the meadows in the bottom of the cages: "Again and again [the lark] would try to hover over that miniature meadow from its miniature sky just underneath the top of the cage. At last, conscience stricken, we carried the beloved prisoner to the meadow west of Dunbar where it was born, and, blessing its sweet heart, bravely set it free, and our exceeding great reward was to see it fly and sing in the sky" (39-40).

It is remarkable how rarely Muir felt the need to editorialize about these comparisons. Usually he merely states them, opposed to each other by their position in the text, as in the example quoted above, and allows the reader to draw his own conclusion about relative values. Muir uses endless variations on this technique to point his own value judgment. His first observation of nature in Wisconsin, a "sudden plash into pure wildness," is contrasted with a discussion of the thrashings he received at the hands of his father (52). Childish games are compared with adult war (30). He tells how the boys sat comfortably on walls with broken glass embedded in the tops, by the simple expedient of piling grass and weeds over the glass, surely a triumph of nature over art (34).

Many other examples could be cited. This book, though it poses as an autobiography, is really a very subversive piece of propaganda. Muir selects those incidents of his youth which best illustrate his favorite theme. Wildness is presented as perfectly beautiful and natural, and then some incident pertaining to civilization, culture, or received religion is contrasted with it. The reader is left to draw his own conclusions, but the manner of presentation leaves little choice.

But Muir is more subtle still. There is a third purpose to each of these incidents: to prepare the reader to accept the change in the last section of the book in the character of John Muir. As an autobiography, *The Story of My Boyhood and Youth* becomes a kind of truthful *bildungsroman* in its last chapters as all of the themes achieve a climax. John's coming of age appears as a result of his childhood influences, his relations with his father, his observations of nature juxtaposed to the evils and inadequacies of civilization. All lead him to the rejection of his father and to the assertion of his own independence.

IV The Education of John Muir

John Muir's education, as detailed in *The Story of My Boyhood and Youth,* was by and large an education into the ways of nature. The books he read were relatively few. He knew the New Testament from Matthew to Revelation "by heart and by sore flesh"; he read much of Shakespeare, Milton, and Cowper; he taught himself the finer points of geometry, algebra, and trigonometry and read what was available in history, biography, and science. He also started early to discipline his body. His

Scotch school in Dunbar was no place for pantywaists. Muir found that his many thrashings in school and at home were "admirably influential in developing . . . fortitude," for if he did not endure his punishment well he was "mocked on the playground, and public opinion on a Scotch playground was a powerful agent in controlling behavior." One of his childhood games was to stand face to face with a comrade and to thrash each other's legs with whips made of stout branches "until one succumbed to the intolerable pain and thus lost the game." The effect was to build a stoic endurance in Muir "that would try anyone but an American Indian" (29-30).

His education in self-reliance continued through his Wisconsin days. After nearly drowning in the lake near his farm, Muir returned to the lake soon afterward, rowed out to the middle, and spent some time diving as deeply as he could. Each time he repeated the process, he shouted aloud, "Take that," like Xerxes whipping the sea. "Never was a victory over self more complete," he concluded (104-5).

His education in nature began correspondingly early. The Scotch children of Dunbar often would compare the number of birds' nests they "kenned," discussing at length the kinds of birds and their comparative difficulty of observation. In the wilds of Wisconsin knowledge of nature came faster. One whole chapter, "A Paradise of Birds," includes lengthy passages about Muir's observations on the loon, the passenger pigeon, and other birds. He also hunted extensively for birds and small game, justifying Thoreau's faith in that pastime as an effective introduction to the woods. (Later in life he never shot a wild creature, even, like Uncle Toby, urging people not to kill spiders and flies.)

One might expect that this kind of education, so at variance with the fundamental religion of Daniel Muir, would bring about the inevitable crisis between father and son, followed by John's first flight on his own wings. Such was not the case. John's schism with his father finally occurred over a much less philosophically satisfying point—the success he achieved with his inventions. John's inventions were a trying-out of his newly acquired self-reliance, of course, but they leave something to be desired as a symbolic fulcrum upon which his later life was to balance. He began working on his inventions because his regimen of early morning reveille turned him loose in a house in which it was too cold to read. To keep warm he whittled wooden clocks, put together "water-wheels, curious doorlocks and latches, thermometers, hygrometers, pyrometers, . . . a barometer, an automatic contrivance for feeding the horses at any required hour, a lamp-lighter and fire-lighter, an early-or-late-rising machine, and so forth" (201). His father only half objected, but in terms which suggest the clash of wills involved:

> "Do you not think it is very wrong to waste your time on such nonsense?"
>
> "No," I said meekly, "I don't think I'm doing any wrong."
>
> "Well," he replied, "I assure you I do; and if you were only half as zealous in the study of religion as you are in contriving and whittling these useless, nonsensical things, it would be infinitely better for you. I want you to be like Paul, who said that he desired to know nothing among men but Christ and Him crucified." (203)

On this unresolved note, unresolved even when Muir wrote of it fifty years later, Muir left his home to exhibit his inventions at the state fair in Madison. The three years 1860-63 are among the most crucial in Muir's life, but are given only a single chapter in *The Story of My Boyhood and Youth*. Muir did, however, include within that one chapter a single incident which reveals, microcosmically, the influences in Madison which shaped his later life. The incident was Muir's first botany lesson, given him, he recollected, by a student named Griswold. Griswold, so states Muir, plucked a leaf from a locust tree and through forcible rhetoric and socratic dialogue led Muir to the realization that a locust tree could be a member of the pea family. The lesson ends with a curious botanical summary supposed to have been given by Griswold: "Now, surely, you cannot imagine that all these similar characters [of the pea and the locust] are mere coincidences. Do they not rather go to show that the Creator in making the pea vine and locust tree had the same idea in mind, and that plants are not classified arbitrarily? Man has nothing to do with their classification. Nature has attended to all that, giving essential unity with boundless variety, so that the botanist has only to examine plants to learn the harmony of their relations" (225). Now I doubt that any student by the name of Griswold[7] or any other except Muir spoke those words. They represent instead a conclusion, or rather two conclusions, reached by Muir during his college years. First, that there is a mystic, Transcendental unity in nature which is somehow revealing of the nature of God, and second, that the study of plants can lead to an understanding of at least certain parts of that unity. Muir learned the Transcendental lesson that to find intuition into the nature of God, one must use one's understanding to realize the nature of nature. The question that goes unanswered in *The Story of My Boyhood and Youth* is how Muir arrived at that conclusion. Surely it was not through the speech of one student botanist, but how was it?

The answer is given in broad outline in Mrs. Jeanne C. Carr's edition of Muir's letters to her, *Letters to a Friend* (1915). Mrs. Carr's influence on Muir seems beyond belief. Undoubtedly it was she who introduced him to the writings of Thoreau and Emerson; it was she who arranged the meeting between Emerson and John Muir in the Yosemite; she who kept faith through his lifetime in his capacity to do good and great things. She was aided in her efforts at Transcendentalizing Muir by the Reverend Walter R. Brooks, a geologist and naturalist as well as a minister, whose sermons on "God in Nature and Life" seem to have exerted a powerful influence on Muir's understanding and interpretation of nature.[8]

Apparently Muir read Emerson and Thoreau thoroughly. Echoes of their prose are common in his writings and his observations are colored by their point of view. Emersonian metaphors abound in *The Story of My Boyhood and Youth*. All the natural perceptions are filtered through a consciousness thoroughly aware of the unity of diversified nature. He sees the flight of passenger pigeons, for example, in a metaphor of a river: "I have seen flocks streaming south in the fall so large that they were flowing over from horizon to horizon in an almost continuous stream all day long, at the rate of forty or fifty miles an hour, like a mighty river in the sky, widening, contracting, descending like falls and cataracts, and rising suddenly here and there in huge ragged masses like high-plashing spray" (128). A discussion of the domestication of animals ends with a comment extending the discussion toward metaphysics: "surely all God's people, however serious and savage, great or small, like to play. Whales and elephants, dancing, humming gnats, and invisibly small mischievous microbes,—all are warm with divine radium and must have lots of fun in them" (150).

Transcendentalism was only one of the influences felt by Muir during his Madison years. More interesting, and more enigmatic, is the question of how, when, and where he first encountered the Darwinian hypothesis that was to have an immense effect upon his writing. The concept of evolution had been widely published by 1860, but in scientific backwaters like a small state college in mid-America, it seems almost inconceivable that a young man, half-educated in botany and thoroughly exposed to the Concord ideas about the unity of nature, should adopt wholeheartedly and vigorously the concept of "nature red in tooth and claw." Muir is remarkable among American Transcendental writers, as I shall show in the next chapter, in his complete acceptance of the implications of evolution. Thoreau seems not to have understood the concept at all, and Emerson's much-quoted couplet from the second epigraph to *Nature*, " 'And striving to be man, the worm/Mounts through all the spires of form'," refers to the concept of the chain of being, not to evolution. Muir alone read, understood, and incorporated the Darwinian ideas into a Transcendental order.

In *The Story of My Boyhood and Youth* Muir barely suggests how important the concepts of evolution became to his mature philosophy. One passage suggests his poised acceptance of a view which was to destroy most Romantic visions of nature. He observes a spirited race between a blowsnake and his intended dinner, a frog. "It was wonderful," he reports dispassionately, "to see how fast the legless, footless, wingless, finless hunter could run." He meditates finally upon the result of such aspects of nature, that having eaten the frog, "while digesting and enjoying his meal, the happy snake would himself be swallowed frog and all by a hawk" (91). Muir does not make a moral extension of this incident to human terms, but, in the description of another incident in which he tells how he had to kill his dog, Watch, because the dog had developed an overpowering appetite for the neighbor chickens, he reveals something more of his feelings about man as "lord of creation": "Think of the millions of squabs that preaching, praying men and women kill and eat, with all sorts of other animals great and small, young and old, while eloquently discoursing on the coming of the blessed peaceful, bloodless millennium!" (68).

V Fact or Fiction?

These themes running through the first section of Muir's autobiography make it a curious mythic, philosophical, and biographical book: mythic, for the story of one boy in conflict with his father parallels the stories of warring and separate generations;

philosophic, for its inherent opposition of revealed religion and the revelation of nature so much a part of John Muir's life. And biographical? A moot question, that, for this is the only work by Muir which is not firmly based on recorded journals which could prove the truth of what is stated in it. Historical records show that the outlines of the story are as Muir presents them, but no reader can take all of this book in stride without pausing a few times to stretch his credulity.

There must be an element of fiction in any biography, I suppose, and particularly in an autobiography written many years after the events recorded. Muir's case is an extreme example, for everything in his later life contradicts the influences exerted on him by his father. All of the philosophic and natural influences of his maturity tended to make him see the events of his boyhood and youth as a patterning or preparation for his life as a naturalist. They probably were nothing of the sort. Muir doubtless rearranged and, yes, invented, where necessary, incidents of his youth which could serve as poignant examples of his predestination as a naturalist. In the interest of verisimilitude, he contrasted these incidents with contrary examples which were far more true to life but less convenient to the legend. Truth will out, however, and the examples of childish cruelty which he included seem far more vivid in this book than the fantasies. The caged skylark, the indignities which Muir heaped upon the family tomcat in Dunbar, the fastening of a snapping turtle to the ear of Muir's dog, Watch, the killing of snakes and hunting in general— all these incidents have the ring of truth. But the less savage events seem less likely. Muir's attempts at apologies for his youthful behavior only give away the game more completely: "The savage in us" (22), "the natural savagery of boys" (23), "a shameful amusement even for wild boys" (66). The weight of evidence suggests that Muir was more at home during his youth attaching snapping turtles to the ears of dogs than observing the pasque-flowers in the fields. The latter interest, having come later in life, is artificially appended to a savage, normal boyhood.

The most violent attack on the reader's willing suspension of disbelief occurs in Muir's description of his train ride from his father's farm to Madison with his armload of inventions for display at the state fair. He first encounters the landlord of the Pardeeville tavern, who immediately notices his bundle of inventions:

"Hello, young man, what's this?"

"Machines," I said, "for keeping time and getting up in the morning, and so forth."

"Well! well! That's a mighty queer get-up. You must be a Down-East Yankee. Where did you get the pattern for such a thing?"

"In my head," I said.   (210)

Next, all the local inhabitants catch sight of the inventions, and crowd around. Muir stands outside the circle and "had the advantage of hearing the remarks without being embarrassed." When a newcomer asks what one of the items is, the tavern-keeper tells him, "Why, a young man that lives out in the country somewhere made it, and he says it's a thing for keeping time, getting up in the morning, and something that I didn't understand. I don't know what he meant." "Oh, no!" one of the crowd would say, "that can't be. Its for something else—something mysterious. Mark my words, you'll see all about it in the newspapers some of these days" (211).

Some of the onlookers invoke phrenology. "I wish I could see that boy's head," Muir reports one of them as saying, "he must have a tremendous bump of invention." Another states that he would rather have Muir's head "than the best farm in the State" (212).

When the train arrives, the conductor is suitably impressed by the inventions, just as the bumpkins of Pardeeville were. He advises Muir to leave the bundle of inventions in the baggage car, for, if he carries them with him, they will surely get broken by the press of the crowd. When Muir asks if he may ride on the engine, the conductor says it will be all right, and convinces the reluctant engineer to allow him. When he arrives at the state fair, he asks for a ticket; but when the ticket-seller sees the bundle, he is allowed through free. The man in charge of the Fine Arts display is equally eager to give him the best display area available and all the help he needs to set up his inventions.

Now, the records show that Muir's inventions made a considerable hit at the fair, that he was indeed catapulted into a sizable local fame at once, but surely no one can read this particular anecdote without sensing that it is, as Mark Twain would say, a "considerable stretcher." No Kafka hero inhabited a world more superreal than the one John Muir tells us he surveyed from Pardeeville to Madison. The scene is an outrageous fantasy on Muir's part. The provocation for it immediately precedes it in *Boyhood*. Muir tells how his father refused to contribute any money to his expedition to Madison, then continues, "Strange to say father carefully taught us to consider ourselves very poor worms of the dust, conceived in sin, etc., and devoutly believed that quenching every spark of pride and self-confidence was a sacred duty. . . . [He] tried to assure me that when I was fairly out in the wicked world making my own way I would soon learn that although I might have thought him a hard taskmaster at times, strangers were far harder" (209-10).

Here was a doctrine that Muir felt he must contradict. Though fond of rambling alone in the woods, he had a natural gregariousness, a love of good friends, that made him despise the coldness of his father's life. As he moved to metaphor to describe his feelings about his father in the matter of chipping the well, so here he turned to a fantastic wish-fulfillment version of events following his departure from "Hickory Hill Farm." Perhaps here again we can see the influence of Emerson, who was no slave to fact either. Truth, John Muir must have felt, could as often be found in metaphor, in fantasy, in exaggeration, as in cold history. The lesson, we shall see, is repeated in his other works.

CHAPTER 2

Naturalist's Progress

I *Would-be Poet*

MUIR SPENT a total of five semesters at the University of Wisconsin, or nearly three years in a milieu totally different from that of his boyhood. Like Melville, he must have "unfolded within himself" many times during that period. Apparently there were occasions when he acted under the influence of his father's harsh moral code, hurling "very orthodox denunciations at all things morally or religiously amiss in old or young," as he wrote when he apologized for his actions later.[1] Much of the time he feared being drafted into the Union Army, and part of his indecision after leaving college resulted from this fear. He was a thoroughgoing pacifist. Though he did some charitable work for the soldiers then in training at Camp Randall in Madison, he was outspoken in his feelings about war: "Were all the secession soldiers safely arranged in rows side by side on long tables, where are the soldiers whose patriotism would enable them calmly or otherwise at such an hour to cut their throats for the commonweal after having asked the married among them how many children they had and if they cried when their pa left them to go to camp."[2]

He was also trying to write during this period, but not very successfully. All his efforts seem to have been in poetry, and are quite varied, in terms of both their tone and their achievement. One, a satiric view of an old log schoolhouse, somewhat in the manner of Cowper, is a fairly successful exercise in an unusual blank verse in which an extra unstressed syllable gives a humorous effect of primitivism in the verse corresponding with the poet's view of the primitive matter of the poem. A few lines will show how the technique works:

> With grammar, too, old schoolhouse, thou hast suffered,
> While Plato, Milton, Shakespeare, have been murdered,

> Torn limb from limb in analytic puzzles,
> And wondrous parsing, passing comprehension,
> The poetry and meaning blown to atoms—
> Sad sacrifices in the glorious cause
> Of higher all-embracing education[3]

He was a little more successful in a lighter narrative poem entitled "In Search of a Breakfast," describing a frustrating search for food on one of Muir's nature walks in Wisconsin. The poem is dedicated to the

> Patron of those luckless brains,
> Which to the wrong side leaning,
> Indite much metre with much pains
> And little or no meaning.[4]

But no one can accuse Muir of "inditing much metre." These two poems and another rather successful imitation of Cowper entitled "The Sabbath" seem to mark the high point of his poetic career.[5] The low point may be seen in a poem in which Muir violated his own feelings about nature to attempt an allegorical effect and was so unsuccessful that he finally broke down into a Bunyanesque prose. Though it is not worth quoting as poetry, it does give an unusual picture of Muir at this age.

> There is a tree of goodly form, and tall
> Among its shapen boughs of strength
> Should frailest zephyr venture, sounds of might
> Skyrending: quick, would rise; o'er all
> Upon the hills, she shouts her songs of worth
> To small eyed trees, and brambles far below
> 'Twas thus I heard her sing when long ago
> I sought an hour of rest beneath her shade.
> "Oh God of trees, ye vines and brambles all
> I pray you listen. List I beseech you
> O listen listen listen Lend your ears
> I do implore you listen listen listen
> And now ye God of trees, brambles and vines
> Give heed I king of trees I'm good
> Ye brambles I am good, I'm good
> Ye vines and God of trees.
> I'm loathe to speak my praise I'm good
> Fruits of all hues are on me, and around
> I bless forever always. And every fruit
> Is on me to bless mankind and brute.

This celebrated tree is nevertheless common. 'Tis always found on uplands, where are also found coarse-grained *'plause* and *poplar breath* upon the high banks of the great river *famecheap* the best specimens are found. Several attempts have been made to introduce it among the groves of noncheery wormwood and light-stomach growing on the lowlands of shortmean and death-trode. But all were unsuccessful as they invariably dropped and died.[6]

Allegory was not Muir's forte, and allegory in which human morality is assigned to plants especially went against his grain. However, the selection marks one of the earliest appearances of Muir's feelings against anthropocentricism—examples of which we shall see later.

In Muir's search for a metier during these years, two desires seem to have been foremost: humanitarianism and inventiveness. When he left Madison in 1863, he fully intended to go to the University of Michigan medical school. However, when he finally did leave Wisconsin, it was to spend time in Canada and Indianapolis putting his inventive powers to work, first in a broom- and rake-handle factory in Meaford, Canada, and later in a carriage equipment factory in Indianapolis. His specific reasons for embarking on these short-lived careers are unknown, but it seems that he was merely temporizing. He could find no real satisfaction in work of this sort, and these occupations were chosen as much to give him time for extensive botanizing in new areas as for any other reason. The termination of this period came through an accident which nearly blinded him but which gave him sufficient time while recuperating to review his life. He concluded that the only way he could find happiness in life would be to make what had been an avocation a vocation. He determined to walk the one-thousand miles from Louisville, Kentucky, to the Gulf of Mexico, botanizing along the way, and, in effect, to become a tramp. He was to be on the side of the angels and Thoreau.

II *Two Forwarding Addresses*

Muir took the train to Louisville; then, on September 2, 1867, he "steered through the big city by compass without speaking a word to anyone" (*A Thousand-Mile Walk*, 247). He had given his brother, Savannah, Georgia, as his forwarding address to send money to him. On his notebook he inscribed another address: "John Muir, Earth-planet, Universe." On this note of ambivalence he began his life in woods and mountains. In one sense he had completely cut himself adrift from home, family, friends, the woods of Wisconsin that he knew and loved so well, and the security of industries who knew how to appreciate his inventive genius. In another sense he stretched a silver cord all the way from Portage, Wisconsin, to Florida and Cuba.

Uncertainty is the most striking aspect of *A Thousand-Mile Walk to the Gulf.* It is a narrative of a man who had not yet made up his mind. Nor did Muir find himself completely until some time after the end of his journey, but within the pages of *A One-Thousand Mile Walk* a careful reader can see what elements went into his decision and how the balance was tipped. He began the narrative with almost perfect ambivalence, noting how he rejoiced "in splendid visions of pines and palms and tropic flowers in glorious array," but "not . . . without a few cold shadows of loneliness" as well (248). At the end of his Southern journey he was still not perfectly sure. He was disappointed with Florida. He had visited it in his dreams, he wrote, in which he "always came suddenly on a close forest of trees, every one in flower, and bent down and entangled to network by luxuriant, bright-blooming vines, and over all a flood of bright sunlight" (315). The reality was disappointing. His first view was of a vast salt marsh, gloomy and nearly impenetrable. He had fantasies about the presence of alligators, and finally came to the frustrating realization that Florida, with all its "plant grandeur so redundant," was so nearly impenetrable that he could only observe it, by and large, like a common tourist, restricted to the edges of high ground (316-17).

But in the process of the journey he also made clear his growing preference for wild nature. He described with scorn the Kentuckyan who would not go ten miles to see Mammoth Cave, "as it was nothing but a hole in the ground" (254). At the cave itself Muir noted the contrast between "Nature's grandeur" and the "paltry artificial gardens" about the hotel (255). When he stayed overnight with a Tennessee farmer, he recorded the next morning that he "escaped from a heap of uncordial kindness to the generous bosom of the woods" (258). Finally, in Florida, after spending a night in the woods and awakening with "flowers and beauty . . . in abundance, but no bread," he stated that "a serious matter is this bread which perishes, and, could it be dispensed with, I doubt if civilization would ever see me again" (321).

Perhaps it was Muir's sojourn in Cuba that tipped the balance toward the wilderness. He marveled continuously at the Cubans, surrounded with natural beauty, yet apparently interested only in violence (365-70). At any rate, by the time he reached New York from Cuba, he was far more at ease in the wilderness than in cities. He stayed in the schooner he arrived in and limited his excursions within the city to the environs of the ship, noting that he dared not adventure so far afield as Central Park, for fear that he could not find his way back. He would have liked to explore the city "if, like a lot of wild hills and valleys, it was clear of inhabitants" (394).

III   *Civil War Documentary*

The principal difference between *A Thousand-Mile Walk* and *The Story of My Boyhood and Youth* is apparent in the different ways Muir treated the theme of choice in each book. *Boyhood and Youth,* written by dictation in his sixties, filtered Muir's experiences of youth through the wisdom he had gained over a lifetime. *A Thousand-Mile Walk,* on the other hand, reflects the immediacy of his experiences, since it is a very slightly edited publication of his journal. This immediacy makes it, in some ways, more of a historical document than a work of art, but in the intensity of Muir's feelings about nature and culture and, as we shall see, in his development of a philosophical *raison d'être*, it becomes almost fiction-like in its organization.

However, it has immense interest as a historical document. Muir was almost perfectly fitted to be a witness of the situation in the South after the Civil War. He was a good observer, and he probably had as much sympathy for the South as anyone in the North. Southern customs, which must have been inconceivable to him, he had the good sense to record objectively. His brief description of one aspect of that fine old Southern custom, the feud, for example, allows the reader to observe the pathos of the situation without forcing him to a moral conclusion. The description, which is one part of a longer section detailing the violence of the postbellum South in general, seems casual enough: "I noticed that a man came regularly after dark to the house for supper. He was armed with a gun, a pistol, and a long knife. My host told me that this man was at feud with one of his neighbors, and that they were prepared to shoot one another on sight. That neither of them could do any regular work or sleep in the same place two nights in succession. That they visited houses only for food, and as soon as the one that I saw had got his supper he went out and slept in the woods, without of course making a fire. His enemy did the same" (278). Muir used much the same kind of innocent eye as Huckleberry Finn's at the Grangerford's, and was rewarded with a similar success.

Many of Muir's comments on Southern customs are marred by a youthful flippancy that is probably a function of his insecurity about his choice of vocation. The *Walk* is spiced with ironic comments summing up contacts with Southern civilization which Muir found meaningful only in terms of his choice of wilderness against culture. Thus an evening spent with a Negro driver in Tennessee is summed up with the pert comment, "received a good deal of knowledge which may be of use should I ever be a negro teamster" (272). Strangely enough, this man who was to become an apostle of the wilderness and of the simple life was also guilty of a supercilious attitude towards the simplicity of existence in the Tennessee mountains. Perhaps the memories of his father's efficiently worked farm in Wisconsin produced his attitude. At any rate, he noticed that the mountaineers did their own spinning and weaving, "wherever the least pretensions are made to thrift and economy," and that "the practice of these ancient arts they deem marks of advancement rather than of backwardness" (276). His ironic summary of the situation is given partly through the words of an old settler:

> This is the most primitive country I have seen, primitive in everything. The remotest hidden parts of Wisconsin are far in advance of the mountain regions of Tennessee and North Carolina. But my host speaks of the "old-fashioned unenlightened times" like a philosopher in the best light of civilization. "I believe in Providence," said he. "Our fathers came into these valleys, got the richest of them, and skimmed off the cream of the soil. The worn-out ground won't yield no roastin' ears now. But the Lord foresaw this state of affairs, and prepared something else for us. And what is it? Why, He meant us to bust open these copper mines and gold mines, so that we may have money to buy the corn that we cannot raise." A most profound observation. (276-77)

Muir's analyses of the situation of the Negroes in the South lack real perception as well. "The negroes of Georgia," he observed, "are extremely mannerly and polite, and appear always to be delighted to find opportunity for obliging anybody" (312). He seems to have no understanding of the oppression that accounts for their behavior, commenting only on exterior appearances: "The negroes here [in Athens, Georgia] have been well trained and are extremely polite. When they come in sight of a white man on the road, off go their hats, even at a distance of forty or fifty yards, and they walk bare-headed until he is out of sight" (288). Possibly his opacity about the Negro problem stems from an unspoken relief from fear of "wild, runaway negroes" (320)—fear of an unknown which may be seen more clearly in his fantastic feelings about alligators. Alligators and Negroes were about equally unknown in the Wisconsin of Muir's youth, and he has vividly described his vague and formless fears about alligators when he arrived in the deep South. Startled by a noise behind him while lunching in a Florida swamp, he fancied he "could feel the stroke of [an alligator's] long notched tail, and could see his big jaws and rows of teeth, closing with a springy snap on me, as I had seen in pictures" (317). The "alligator" turned out to be a white crane, "handsome as a minister from spirit land," and Muir's fear subsided. Muir seemed to have similar fears about other aspects of this new part of the world he was exploring. "The South has plant fly-catchers," he observed. "It also has plant man-catchers" (268). Such an inhospitable area might provide animal and even human dangers as well.

Muir encountered several dangerous humans (none of them Negroes) during his thousand-mile walk, and came off rather well. An encounter with a roving band of guerrillas who, "long accustomed to plunder, deplored the coming of peace" (269), caused him a few anxious moments but no violence. Another man who intended to rob him changed his mind when he discovered that Muir's bag held only "a comb, brush, towel, soap, a change of underclothing, a copy of Burns' poems, Milton's Paradise Lost, and a small New Testament" (260). These evidences of post-war lawlessness stand alone in the book, except for one other comment on the effect of the war on the South, this one clothed in a metaphor from nature:

> The traces of war are apparent not only on the broken fields, burnt fences, mills, and woods ruthlessly slaughtered, but also on the countenances of the people. A few years after a forest

has been burned another generation of bright and happy trees arises, in purest, freshest vigor; only the old trees, wholly or half dead, bear marks of the calamity. So with the people of the war-field. Happy, unscarred, and unclouded youth is growing up around the aged, half-consumed, and fallen parents, who bear in sad measure the ineffaceable marks of the farthest-reaching and most infernal of all civilized calamities.   (313)

IV   *Fact or Fiction, Once Again.*

There is much less question of the factual nature of the *Walk* than there is of *The Story of My Boyhood and Youth.* Edited by William Frederick Badé from the journal made during the walk, it reflects, by and large, Muir's immediate experience. Still, one cannot but feel that Muir has arranged certain experiences to achieve a maximum literary effect. An entanglement with thorny plant "man-catchers" is followed immediately by his encounter with the guerrilla band, and both are described in retrospect. When his mood is weary, his natural surroundings reflect his weariness almost too perfectly. He seems to have understood perfectly well the literary effectiveness of the "pathetic fallacy." Muir also asserts a kind of order to his experiences which surely was not present, at least to the same degree, in life. His arrival at the seacoast, with the accompanying "scent of the salt sea breezes" reminds him of his boyhood in Dunbar. The thoughts of youth, in turn, reflect his joyousness at having arrived nearly at the end of his journey. Then, all these happy sensations are brought into immediate contrast with a sickness which follows hard upon them. All of the events are real enough—Muir's arrival at the Atlantic and his subsequent attack of malaria—but, in the recording of them in the journal, a literary intelligence has brought order and process into the chaotic impressions of life.

This technique of Muir's can be inordinately subtle. Sometimes the effect he achieves is symphonic: a statement of theme, elaboration, then possibly a variation upon it. One example should show how the technique works. The cypress forests of Georgia create in him a mood of gloomy wonder. "The winds are full of strange sounds, making one feel far from the people and plants and fruitful fields of home," he begins, possibly self-consciously poetic with his use of alliteration. Then he elaborates with an example from his own experiences: "Night is coming on and I am filled with indescribable loneliness. Felt feverish; bathed in a black silent stream, nervously watchful for alligators." After a brief interlude of botanical description, still largely somber in tone but more suggestive of the sublimity of nature, he concludes the passage with a comic variation on the theme: "Met a young African with whom I had a long talk. Was amused with his eloquent narrative of coon hunting, alligators, and many superstitions. He showed me a place where a railroad train had run off the track, and assured me that the ghosts of the killed may be seen every dark night" (293). Then, the mood having been explored sufficiently, and artistically concluded by the Negro's comic relief, Muir is free to go on to a new incident in a different tone.

Muir has the best of both artistic worlds: his journals reflect the immediacy of life as he is experiencing it, yet are governed by a controlling consciousness that gives them an artistic form. It seems almost an ideal way to write, partaking of all of the advantages of both fiction and autobiography with few of the disadvantages. Thoreau is the master of the form, but Muir is hardly less successful in employing it. But Thoreau had one advantage over Muir—he was far less a man of action than was Muir, and in Thoreau's creation of the single character, himself, in his great work, he had less of the purely fictional problem of representing his own heroic action in a credible way. I suppose that viewed either way, as autobiography or as fiction, the representation of a man invariably successful in his pursuits would soon be cloying, but even the hint of fiction in such an autobiography would be intolerable. Muir's writings, from this point of view, do at times become enervating.

Perhaps the best example of this effect occurs in the description of his trip from Florida to Cuba. Muir describes the mounting storm at sea in mixed landsman's and seaman's terms: "In less than a day our norther increased in strength to the storm point. Deeper and wider became the valleys, and yet higher the hills of the round plain of water. The flying jib and gaff topsails were lowered and mainsails close-reefed, and our deck was white with broken wave tops." Then he reports his reaction to the storm with doubtful verisimilitude: " 'You had better go below,' said the captain. 'The Gulf Stream, opposed by this wind, is raising a heavy sea and you will be sick. No landsman can stand this long.' I replied that I hoped the storm would be as violent as his ship could bear, that I enjoyed the scenery of such a sea so much that it was impossible to be sick, that I had long waited in the woods for such a storm, and that, now that the precious thing had come, I would remain on deck and enjoy it. 'Well,' said he, 'if you can stand this, you are the first landsman I ever saw that could.' "[7]

Now, even James Fenimore Cooper had enough respect for appearances concerning the character of Natty Bumppo that he refused to let him behave as heroically at sea as he does on land. In *The Pathfinder*, though Natty does not get seasick (can anyone imagine Natty Bumppo retching over a rail?), Cooper carefully points out that Natty's "gifts" are not such that his heroism can prevail on the water. Muir, possibly acting under the assumption that "truth" allows him greater tolerance in the reader's credibility, naïvely details his ability to withstand the effects of a ship's motion. He does, however, tactfully shift the emphasis from his personal capacity to withstand a natural effect heroically by discussing in detail (and in landsman's language) the order which he finds in the violent sea: "my attention was mostly directed among the glorious fields of foam-topped waves. . . . I could see no striving in those magnificent wave-motions, no raging; all the storm was apparently inspired with nature's beauty and harmony" (362-63). The shift of emphasis helps, but it is not quite enough. Muir has almost too much control over himself, is too much attuned to his environment. As we shall see, the problem is rather a persistent one in his writing.

V *The Metamorphosis of a Naturalist.*

If Muir had not chosen his vocation when he began his one-thousand mile walk, he had when he ended it. The change in his personality was deep and far-reaching. Not that this volume is his *Walden*. The comparison with Thoreau, helpful as it is, is misleading in that no one of Muir's books can be considered as crucial to his development as *Walden* was to Thoreau. Still, if the *Thousand Mile Walk* is not Muir's *Walden*, it does represent something like Thoreau's "Higher Laws" chapter. In this volume Muir, for the first time, began his formulation of the meaning of nature, the position of man in nature, and his own moral obligation concerning that position.

The formulation, neither in what Muir observed nor in his analysis of it, is simple. Muir is both too careful an observer and too much a mystic to make the mistake of acceding simplicity of any sort to nature. To suggest this complexity, Muir used an image for the first time in this work which he repeated often in his later writings—the image of the palimpsest:

> When a page is written over but once it may be easily read; but if it be written over and over with characters of every size and style, it soon becomes unreadable, although not a single confused meaningless mark or thought may occur among all the written characters to mar its perfection. Our limited powers are similarly perplexed and overtaxed in reading the inexhaustible pages of nature, for they are written over and over uncountable times, written in characters of every size and color, sentences composed of sentences, every part of a character a sentence. There is not a fragment in all nature, for every relative fragment of one thing is a full harmonious unit in itself. All together form the one grand palimpsest of the world.   (376-77)

I suppose the first point to note in this passage is the Transcendental tone. The pun on the word "sentence" in particular is Thoreauvian, while the concept of "each in all" of the last two sentences is thoroughly Emersonian, as is the total concept of the overwritten marks of nature in comparison with the palimpsest. But underlying these observations is the more important conclusion manifest in the passage—Muir *chooses* to read nature in its fullness and as a metaphor for all of life. The passage represents a value judgment, or rather, two value judgments superimposed. Muir will study nature, and he will study its diversity with the hope, nay, the assurance, of finding after all a fundamental unity within it. Only by overcoming the "perplexity" which the face of nature presents to its student, he says, can an understanding of its unity be gained.

This value judgment and decision represent a conclusion made by Muir. We might properly expect to see within the pages of this volume the steps by which he arrived at it. The steps are indeed there, clearly set forth and available for the careful reader to follow. They represent, by and large, a rethinking by Muir of the problem of man's position in creation. He begins with an observation which might have come right out of Shelley, or even the derangement of Roderick Usher, concerning the sensitivity of plants to humans in their environment. Muir noted that Schrankia vines growing in traveled places were "much less sensitive" than those growing in more secluded areas. "How little we know as yet of the life of plants," he expostulates, "their hopes and fears, pains and enjoyments!" (261-62).

Somewhat later, when he observes his first palmetto, he is still unsure of the capacity of plants to feel, but is more certain that they have powers of expression which the initiate may observe. "Whether rocking and rustling in the wind or poised thoughtfully and calm in the sunshine," the palmetto, Muir observed, "has a power of expression not excelled by any plant high or low." Though he has been told that "plants are perishable, soulless creatures, that only man is immortal," he concludes that the palmetto "told me grander things than I ever got from human priest" (319). Implicit in his observation is the idea that man is less important than he thinks, particularly in comparison with such vegetable grandeur as the palmetto. The idea is made explicit a little later in a comparison of man with some of the grasses of the Florida swamps. Though he uses Whitman's symbol of grass for the ubiquity of creation, he uses it in a manner peculiar to his own observations about the relative importance of vegetable nature and man: "How strangely we are blinded to beauty and color, form and motion, by comparative size! For example, we measure grasses by our own stature and by the height and bulkiness of trees. But what is the size of the greatest man, or the tallest tree that ever overtopped a grass! Compared with other things in God's creation the difference is nothing. We are only microscopic animalcula" (327).

Here is a new kind of relativity placing man in a more proper perspective with his surroundings. This "lord of creation," Muir finds, is, like the grasses and trees, small potatoes when seen in the context of nature at large. More, man has not the capacity for bloom and color that the flowers have, nor does he show to Muir the orderly processes of change observable in a plant's life cycle. Has Muir gone too far? He goes still farther. After all, in these selections he was considering man only in relation to plants; in comparisons with wild animals Muir becomes even more outspoken in his criticisms of man's supposed place in the order of nature. He considers the alligator at length, first in terms of the common Floridian's opinion: "Many good people believe that alligators were created by the devil, thus accounting for their all-consuming appetite and ugliness." Muir does not agree with that opinion, implying as it does, heretically, a Manichaean order of nature. He finds alligators "beautiful in the eyes of God," however "fierce and cruel they appear to us";

and he accounts for them at length in a curious synthesis of the Darwinian influence upon him compounded with a portion of his father's fundamentalism:

> The antipathies existing in the Lord's great family must be wisely planned like balanced repulsion and attraction in the mineral kingdom. How narrow we selfish, conceited creatures are in our sympathies! how blind to the rights of all the rest of creation! With what dismal irreverence we speak of our fellow mortals! Though alligators, snakes, etc., naturally repel us, they are not mysterious evils. They dwell happily in these flowery wilds, are part of God's family, unfallen, undepraved, and cared for with the same species of tenderness and love as is bestowed on angels in heaven or saints on earth.   (324)

Too far yet? There is more. After noting that he thinks better of alligators now that he has seen them in their home,[8] Muir ends his discussion of them with this lovely peroration: "Honorable representatives of the great saurians of an older creation, may you long enjoy your lilies and rushes, and be blessed now and then with a mouthful of terror-stricken man by way of dainty!" (324-25).

It is very doubtful that a thoroughgoing Humanist would enjoy Muir's writings very much. This volume, which was not published during his lifetime, is his most outspoken anti-anthropocentric writing, but the concept is central to, or implicit in, most of his ideas. His greatest contempt is for the concept that nature is provided for man's use; Muir exceeds even Emerson, who accepted "commodity" as an important use of nature. His opinion of hunting we might guess: "To me it appeared as 'd----dest' work to slaughter God's cattle for sport. 'They were made for us,' say these self-approving preachers; 'for our food, our recreation, or other uses not yet discovered.' As truthfully we might say on behalf of a bear, when he deals successfully with an unfortunate hunter, 'Men and other bipeds were made for bears, and thanks be to God for claws and teeth so long'" (342-43).

Certainly the most important effect the one-thousand-mile walk had on Muir was to convince him that he was on the side of nature in any conflict with man. He ends his discussion of the Humanist's concept of hunting with a peroration even more outspokenly ironic than the one in praise of alligators:

> Let a Christian hunter go to the Lord's woods and kill his well-kept beasts, or wild Indians, and it is well; but let an

enterprising specimen of these proper, predestined victims go to houses and fields and kill the most worthless person of the vertical godlike killers,—oh! that is horribly unorthodox, and on the part of the Indians atrocious murder! Well, I have precious little sympathy for the selfish propriety of civilized man, and if a war of races should occur between the wild beasts and Lord Man I would be tempted to sympathize with the bears. (343)

Such outbursts are only one side of the development of Muir's ideas on these subjects: the immediate emotional reaction against human nature by a man constitutionally adapted to favor wild nature. The walk gave Muir time to reflect at greater leisure and philosophic distance on the same phenomena, and he used the opportunity to clarify his own feelings in much less emotive terms than the ones quoted above. Apparently the contrast he felt between the comfort of the temperate zones he was used to and the discomfort he felt in the semi-tropic regions of Florida struck him forcibly, for he begins his most balanced discussion of anthropocentrism with an analysis of Florida's climate, and then he uses the same climate as a central image in the discussion. Florida was wracked with diseases, he noted, from constant malaria to "plagues of cholera and yellow fever that come and go suddenly like storms, prostrating the population and cutting gaps in it like hurricanes in woods." The phenomenon needs explanation, and Muir attempts it: "The world, we are told, was made especially for man—a presumption not supported by all the facts. A numerous class of men are painfully astonished whenever they find anything living or dead, in all God's universe, which they cannot eat or render in some way what they call useful to themselves."

Such men, to Muir, are simply heretics: "It is hardly possible to be guilty of irreverence in speaking of *their* God any more than of heathen idols." What kind of God do such men create? He is, naturally, anthropomorphic and highly pragmatic. "He is regarded as a civilized, law-abiding gentleman in favor either of a republican form of government or of a limited monarchy; believes in the literature and language of England; is a warm supporter of the English constitution and Sunday schools and missionary societies; and is as purely a manufactured article as any puppet of a half-penny theater." It is remarkable that both the diction and the irony of this passage, written in 1867, are quite similar to the later writings of Mark Twain. Like Twain,

Muir holds such a position in purest contempt. But his contempt is centered on opinions concerning wild nature, not primarily on social evils, as was Twain's. He is not surprised that the vision of nature included in such beliefs is as much in error as the vision of God in society. "To such properly trimmed people, the sheep, for example, is an easy problem—food and clothing 'for us,' eating grass and daisies white by divine appointment for his predestined purpose, on perceiving the demand for wool that would be occasioned by the eating of the apple in the Garden of Eden."

He continues the catalog. Whales are merely "storehouses of oil for us"; hemp is destined only for "ship's rigging, wrapping packages, and hanging the wicked"; cotton must have been "intended" for clothing; iron for hammers and ploughs; and, most ironically, "lead for bullets, all intended for us." Now, when such a view of nature encounters those objects which do not fit into the plan—"lions, tigers, alligators—which smack their lips over raw man" and the "myriads of noxious insects that destroy [man's] labor and drink [man's] blood," Muir poses the ironically innocent question: "Doubtless man was intended for food and drink for all these?" He answers it as the anthropo-centrist would: "Oh, no! Not at all! These are unresolvable difficulties connected with Eden's apple and the Devil." "Why does water drown its lord? Why do so many minerals poison him? Why are so many plants and fishes deadly enemies?" And, most tellingly, "Why is the lord of creation subject to the same laws of life as his subjects?" Muir gives the anthropocentric answer again: such anomalies are somehow connected with the devil or the loss of paradise.

His own answer is a combination of the doctrine of plenitude in the "chain of being" concept and man's situation in relation to evolution. "Nature's object in making animals and plants," he finds, is "first of all the happiness of each one of them, not the creation of all for the happiness of one." Why, he asks, "should man value himself as more than a small part of the one great unit of creation?" Only the concept of plenitude is satisfying to him: "what creature of all that the Lord has taken the pains to make is not essential to the completeness of that unit—the cosmos? The universe would be incomplete without man; but it would also be incomplete without the smallest transmicroscopic creature that dwells beyond our conceitful eyes and knowledge." Like Emerson, he believes that "All are needed by each one/

Nothing is fair or good alone." His feeling about the position of God in relation to evolution and man's position in nature is fairly mechanical. God, he seems to say, kept the evolutionary process going, without any intent at all to suggest that man is any better than any other of his fellow creatures, or even better than the plants or non-organic compounds. Muir admits his own uncertainty in this matter, but he points out that no one else is more certain, though many say that they are. Mortality seems to be his only criterion for sympathy. "From the dust of the earth, from the common elementary fund, the Creator has made *Homo sapiens.* From the same material he has made every other creature, however noxious and insignificant to us. They are earthborn companions and fellow mortals." Later he even questions the criterion of mortality: "Plants are credited with but dim and uncertain sensation, and minerals with positively none at all. But why may not even a mineral arrangement of matter be endowed with sensation of a kind that we in our blind exclusive perfection can have no manner of communication with?" The implication is that even minerals have his sympathy.

All this may seem a *reductio ad absurdum* of his own position; Muir certainly cut plants and pressed them, and he chipped rocks when he needed to gain footholds for his climbing. Is he not then guilty of failing to live by his own code? I do not think so, for Muir is here stating an extreme position in opposition to what he considers an even more extreme position. Also, he *lived* his rejection of society, with its pragmatic concept of nature; never forget his regret that the necessity of the "bread which perishes" was the only source which bound him to civilization. He cannot deal intellectually with a problem which is primarily an emotional one for the mass of men; he must take a defensive position: "The fearfully good, the orthodox, of this laborious patchwork of modern civilization cry 'Heresy' on every one whose sympathies reach a single hair's breadth beyond the boundary epidermis of our own species. Not content with taking all of earth, they also claim the celestial country as the only ones who possess the kind of souls for which that imponderable empire was planned."

Muir's position is a kind of heresy, according to orthodox Christianity, when stated that way. It is one thing to believe in the sentience of plants and minerals, another to believe that animals have souls and are capable of regeneration. He writes here as a dialectician. The "imponderable empire," heaven, is denied all save believing man by the orthodox, although absolutely nothing is known empirically about it. The orthodox use empirical argument when it is convenient, dismiss it when it is not. Not fair, says Muir. "This star, our own good earth, made many a successful journey around the heavens ere man was made, and whole kingdoms of creatures enjoyed existence and returned to dust ere man appeared to claim them. After human beings have also played their part in Creation's plan, they too may disappear without any general burning or extraordinary commotion whatever." If that be heresy, he implies, make the most of it. The evidence of evolution bears out the first part and suggests (before man gained the power to destroy all of nature on earth with himself) the last.

No, concludes Muir, it is unfair of man to see things with such an intricate double vision, to keep two sets of books to account for nature as commodity and nature as red in tooth and claw. Unquestionably, "venomous beasts, thorny plants, and deadly diseases of certain parts of the earth prove that the whole world was not made for [man]." The efforts of orthodox apologists to "accuse the first mother of the cause of the difficulty" or to see these apparent evils as "a providential chastisement for some self-invented form of sin" simply will not hold water. Nor does nature, whether in the form of "uneatable and uncivilized animals" or the most beautiful flowers, "require the cleansing chemistry of universal planetary combustion." But Muir is willing to apply that combustion to man: "More than aught else mankind requires burning, as being in great part wicked, and if that transmundane furnace can be so applied and regulated as to smelt and purify us into conformity with the rest of the terrestrial creation, then the tophetization of the erratic genus *Homo* were a consummation devoutly to be prayed for." Here indeed is misanthropy brought to its logical extension. Man, instead of being the lord of creation, is possibly saved from God's wrath only by the impracticality of wasting the rest of creation by the destruction of all. The alligator and the staphylococcus, far from being creatures of the devil and the enemy of man, are, in their simple goodness, insurance against our destruction! Can there be any wonder why Muir took to the Sierra? "Glad to leave these ecclesiastical fires and blunders," he concludes the discussion, "I joyfully return to the immortal truth and immortal beauty of Nature."

VI *Transcendence*

The passage discussed at length above (*A Thousand-Mile Walk*, 354-58) is Muir's longest and most complete discussion of his personal theology. It should be noted that it is almost entirely defensive, negative. What of positive statements beyond the hopeful, "I joyfully return to the immortal truth and immortal beauty of Nature?" It might be answered that all of *A Thousand Mile Walk to the Gulf* is a positive statement by Muir, that his life as he lived it after this period illustrates his choice. But more specific affirmations are given profusely in the volume. Assertions are made quietly, almost casually, perhaps giving even better testimony to Muir's willingness to comprehend (in the double sense of that word) nature. For example, Muir has quiet confidence in the order of nature in his simple assertion about the growth of the agave, as he observed it in Cuba: "This plant is said to make a mighty effort to flower and mature its seeds and then to die of exhaustion. Now there is not, so far as I have seen, a mighty effort or the need of one, in wild Nature. She accomplishes her ends without unquiet effort" (378).

But the most positive assertion by Muir of his desire for a life in nature appears at the end of his thousand-mile walk in a passage that was apparently written at a period of greater leisure than most of the entries in the book. Aboard the schooner that was to take him to New York, he meditated at length at first upon that constant in nature, the wind; and then in a summary he reflects upon all that he felt he had learned during his walk to the gulf. The passage (*A Thousand-Mile Walk*, 384-91) is a blend of Emersonian reflection and metaphor plus the natural sensibility typical of Muir.

The meditation on the wind is the most apparently Emersonian one in this book. Muir begins by noting that Christ told Nicodemus that he "did not know where the winds came from nor where they were going," and that modern science had not improved much or at all upon the knowledge of "those Palestinian Jews." He then continues at length: "The substance of the winds is too thin for human eyes, their written language is too difficult for human minds, and their spoken language mostly too faint for human ears. A mechanism is said to have been invented whereby the human organs of speech are made to write their own utterances. But without any extra mechanical contrivance, every speaker also writes as he speaks. All things in the creation of God register their own acts. The poet was mistaken when he said, 'From the wing no scar the sky sustains.' His eyes were simply too dim to see the scar. In sailing past Cuba I could see a fringe of foam along the coast, but could hear no sound of waves, simply because my ears could not hear wave-dashing at that distance. Yet every bit of spray was sounding in my ears" (384-85). The metaphor from mechanics, the progression of paradoxes, the diction in general might as well be Emerson's as Muir's but the sensibility—"every bit of spray was sounding in my ears"—is entirely Muir's own.

The subject then reminds Muir of the variety of winds he has encountered during his walk, and the quality of wind is suddenly transformed into a symbol of ubiquity in nature, like the grass in Whitman's "Song of Myself." From Indiana to the Gulf, he noted, "earth and sky, plants and people" were constantly changing. Nature and man, a few miles apart, in Kentucky had "many a characteristic shibboleth," different flower faces, different architecture of barns and cabins. But in spite of the apparent changes, Muir found two unifying factors: "I noted no difference in the sky, and the winds spoke the same things. I did not feel myself in a strange land."

In Tennessee, North Carolina, and Georgia the feeling of change persisted. He reports, "my known flower companions were leaving [me] now not one by one . . . but in whole tribes and genera, and companies of shining strangers came trooping upon me in countless ranks." But it was not until the character of the sky and wind changed that he really began to feel himself "a stranger in a strange land." Florida "delighted, astonished, confounded" him with its vegetation, surely, but even more in the change in "tone and language of the winds. They no longer came with the old home music gathered from open prairies and waving fields of oak, but they passed over many a strange string. The leaves of magnolia, smooth like polished steel, the immense inverted forests of tillandsia banks, and the princely crowns of palms—upon these the winds made strange music, and at the coming-on of night had overwhelming power to present the distance from friends and home, and the completeness of my isolation from all things familiar" (387).

Wind functions for Muir as both a unifying and a diversifying symbol. It is ubiquitous and constant, yet it is subtly different in different places. He emphasizes this aspect by recalling how the first scent of a sea-breeze in Georgia reminded him of his youth in Scotland: "I was plodding along with my satchel and plants, leaning wearily forward, a little sore from approaching fever, when suddenly I felt the salt air, and before I had time to think, a whole flood of long-dormant associations rolled in upon me. The Firth of Forth, The Bass Rock, Dunbar Castle, and the winds and rocks and hills came upon the wings of that wind, and stood out in as clear and sudden light as a landscape flashed upon the view of a blaze of lightning in a dark night" (387). Thus wind, a constant but ever changing feature of nature, has the power to invoke to individual sensibilities personal and deeply felt reactions.

One can easily detect the stream-of-consciousness transition from these meditations on the wind, replete with feelings of unity with nature and, conversely, a sense of the strangeness of his situation which led Muir to the final matter of observation. He shifts immediately from the salt breeze which reminded him of Scotland to his current situation aboard the schooner. The latter observation gives him an opportunity to express his delight in his nearness to the wildness of wind: "I like to cling to a small chip of a ship like ours when the sea is rough, and long, comet-tailed streamers are blowing from the curled top of every wave." A big ship lumbers unevenly in cross waves, while a small ship, like the one he was on, "glides up one side and down the other of each wave hill in delightful rhythm." His mood becomes more lyric as he proceeds until he is drawn into a metaphor of Christ that is still completely his own in its intense absorption with nature and his love for it:

> I almost forgot at times that the glassy, treeless country was forbidden to walkers. How delightful it would be to ramble over it on foot, enjoying the transparent crystal ground, and the music of its rising and falling hillocks, unmarred by the ropes and spars of a ship; to study the plants of these waving plains and their stream-currents; to sleep in wild weather in a bed of phosphorescent wave-foam, or briny scented seaweeds; to see the fishes by night in pathways of phosphorescent light; to walk the glassy plain in calm, with birds and flocks of glittering fishes here and there, or by night with every star pictured in its bosom! (388-89)

VII *Drang nach Westen*

With his mind full of lyric meditations like the one just quoted, Muir was not ready to return to the civilization he knew, let alone the even more artificial pastures and canyons of New York

City which, as he wrote, he would like to explore if it were "clear of inhabitants" (394). Still, the semi-tropic climate and herbage of Florida kept him alien to its real nature—remained esoteric to him in spite of his growing familiarity with it. His mind made up about the relative values of wild nature and civilization, only one path lay open to him.

Mr. R. W. B. Lewis has catalogued the literary effects of the phenomenon whose cultural symptom in American life is summed up in Greeley's famous phrase, "Go West, young man." Mr. Lewis also associates the westward attraction with Edenic qualities. The Christian overtones of the passage from Muir quoted above are perhaps not superfluous; it is likely that Muir felt himself to be, at least to his own self-consciousness, a new Adam, and had thoughts of Eden as he bought his passage to California. No Eastern or Midwestern "Aunt Pollies" would "sivilize" him, he determined; but, like all of the rebels of American literature, he too would "light out for the territories." Indeed, one can perhaps see this peculiar manifestation of American Romanticism (essentially, Transcendentalism) in its purest form in Muir. Unself-conscious as a writer (although the keeping of a journal would seem to presuppose its eventual publication), he "lit out for the territories" simply to live his life to the fullest in perfect emulation of Thoreau. No less than Thoreau, Muir's "profession was living"; but, unlike Thoreau, who considered himself quite a traveler in Concord, Muir felt the need to travel to the end of this continent in hope of discovering an Eden truer even than Walden Pond. His passage westward must seem inevitable by any standards, once the decision implicit in *A Thousand-Mile Walk to the Gulf* had been made.

CHAPTER *3*

First Summer in the Sierra

O N MARCH 28, 1868, John Muir arrived in San Francisco
via the Isthmus of Panama from New York. He stayed one
day in San Francisco, then enquired of a townsman the nearest
way out of town. "Where do you want to go," he was asked,
and he replied, "to any place that is wild."[1]

But escaping from the confines of civilization is not quite that
easy, as Muir soon learned; there is, inevitably, the problem of
"the bread that perishes." Muir's first year in California was
spent largely in the lowlands. He was able to walk through the
San Joaquin Valley and at least to see briefly the high Sierra
and the Yosemite, but he soon ran out of money and food and
was forced to return to the foothills. He temporized his burning
desire to live in the mountains for several months before his
first opportunity arose.

These months spent, like those of Moses in frustrating contemplation of a nearby holy land, were most important to Muir's
development as a writer and to his final decision concerning the
choice between civilization and wild nature. He has left two
curiously dissimilar accounts of this period. "Twenty Hill
Hollow," first published in *The Overland Monthly* for July,
1872, and reprinted in a slightly revised form by Badé in *A
Thousand-Mile Walk to the Gulf*, is a self-consciously literary
travelogue. In it, Muir as a person has almost been erased; the
essay includes few personal experiences and presents instead
a generalized picture of the topography of the foothills near the
mouth of the Merced River and suggests in general terms the
spiritual sensations of life close to the mountains. A very personal journal of these months, from which the essay "Twenty
Hill Hollow" was drawn, is printed by Linnie Marsh Wolfe in
John of the Mountains (1-33). A comparison of the two accounts

gives an unusual insight into Muir as a mountaineer and Muir as a Transcendental philosopher and writer.

I   *The Eagle in the Hollow*

I hope I have not given the impression in the discussion of Muir's two books about his life before his arrival in California that he was a disciplined writer. I have tried to show that *The Story of My Boyhood and Youth* and, to a lesser extent, *A Thousand-Mile Walk* are, in spite of the eccentric digressions in the former and the apparent casualness of the latter, somewhat thematically organized. However, in neither of these books is an artistic conscience especially noticeable; and, in my efforts to show that each book makes *some* effort, conscious or unconscious, to achieve art, I would not want to suggest that this ordering process is entirely successful. Rather, it must be exhumed from contrary and non-artistic appearances. That situation is entirely changed in the third volume (chronologically) of Muir's spiritual autobiography, *My First Summer in the Sierra*. In that book, Muir successfully represents symbols of a cultural-natural struggle that raise the work to the level of art. The two versions of the time spent before that first summer in the Sierra present a microcosm, as it were, of the more sustained effort represented by his third book.

Muir began his journal of life at "Smoky Jack's Sheep Camp" with a recapitulation, written sometime later, of the events occurring before January 1, 1869, the first dated entry in the journal.[2] The section describes his brief trip to Yosemite, a wandering, uncharted trip—"A strong butterfly full of sunshine settles not long at any place" (2). He then describes in broad strokes and with flippant humor how he found employment as a shepherd. One does not read very far into the passage before discovering that Muir is self-consciously trying out his wings as a writer in this journal. He includes a conversation with the shepherd he is relieving in much more detail than any of the conversations in *A Thousand-Mile Walk;* he revels in a detailed description of the sordid cabin in which he must sleep; he attempts a simile: the sheep "came crowding out, gushing and squeezing like water escaping from a broken flume" (4); his first effort at baking sourdough bread elicits an attempt at self-ironic humor: "I began to hope that like Goodyear I had discovered a new article of manufacture" (5). He even falls victim to a kind of poetic diction, which he had previously escaped, when he describes the sheep herd as a "felted phalanx." He attempts to excuse a cliché by apologizing for it: "The night was what is usually called wild and dismal" (7). This section of the journal is, all in all, a remarkable production, revealing, in a way that the relatively unself-conscious journal of the one-thousand mile walk never did, his comparative youth and inexperience as a writer.

Once back on the firm ground of daily journal entries, his writing is far more successful. Entry follows upon entry, describing the events of each day, and each is selected and expanded or reduced as the material and its importance warrant. Important themes and subjects are similar to those found in *A Thousand-Mile Walk*: anti-anthropocentrism, the palimpsest of nature, God's love for all plants and animals, etc. With a few notable exceptions (which I will discuss shortly), this journal is almost identical in subject and manner to the *Thousand-Mile Walk*.

But it is what Muir made of these journal entries a few years later when he wrote "Twenty Hill Hollow" that is most interesting. The technique can be seen in his handling of one incident recorded in the journal under the date of January 2, 1869, and turned into a central image for the essay. In the journal Muir noted how an eagle landed on one of the hills near his flock of sheep. "At first," he observed, "I could not guess what could bring this strong sailor of the sky to the ground. His great wings, seven or eight feet broad, were folded as he stood, dim, motionless, and clod-like as if all excelsior instincts—all of cloud and sky—were forgotten and that, lark-like, he meant to walk about in the grass hereafter, or stand on a hillock, like the little burrowing owl. But as I watched him attentively, the cause of his earthiness became apparent. Food, which brings both eagles and men from the clouds, was a-wanting—he hungered and came down for a hare" (9).

The description of the eagle in the journal is full of the suggestion that Muir identified himself with the bird. But, when he came to revise the anecdote for the essay on "Twenty Hill Hollow," he boldly deleted all of the excess of the passage to make the description most significant in the essay, abstracting it, and pointing out its symbolic value. It becomes there, "The eagle does not dwell in the Hollow; he only floats there to hunt the long-eared hare" (*Walk*, 406). The poetic concision and abstraction of the statement is haunting, as Muir intended it to be. The concept is taken up again in the concluding paragraph of the essay, describing the distant Sierra Nevada range:

> It may be asked, What have mountains fifty or a hundred miles away to do with Twenty Hill Hollow? To lovers of the wild, these mountains are not a hundred miles away. Their spiritual power and the goodness of the sky make them near, as a circle of friends. They rise as a portion of the hilled walls of the Hollow. You cannot feel yourself out of doors; plain, sky, and mountains ray beauty which you feel. You bathe in these spirit-beams, turning round and round, as if warming at a camp-fire. Presently you lose consciousness of your own separate existence: you blend with the landscape, and become part and parcel of nature. (*Walk,* 416)

Here is perhaps the best example in all of Muir's writing of the use of real incident, abstracted and generalized, to produce a Transcendental identification with nature.

II *Some Themes, Old and New*

The journal kept at Smoky Jack's sheep camp reads much like a continuation of *A Thousand-Mile Walk,* and it should be remembered that it follows immediately upon that earlier journal. Most of the themes of the earlier journal are still present. For example, Muir is still on the side of animals and against man, even to the point of recording his own derelictions in that direction. When he impulsively kills a rattlesnake by jumping on him, he notes revealingly that the snake, "defended himself bravely and I ought to have been bitten. He was innocent and deserved life" (*John of the Mountains,* 28).

Perhaps more important are his observations on coyotes, for here Muir suffered from a perfect Transcendental ambivalence: his body had contracted for the care of the sheep in his herd; his soul favored the freedom and ranging power of the coyote. He says of the coyotes that "they are beautiful animals, and, though cursed of man, are loved of God. Their sole fault is that they are fond of mutton" (14). And again, upon observing a coyote on the outskirts of the herd, he drives it away; but he reflects in his journal later: "I did not make any allowance for his morning hunger, but almost wished I had not seen him, that he might have had a lamb in peace. The flower hungers and watches for the sunshine, the sparrow for the grass seeds, and the wolf for the sheep" (18).

The palimpsest image, which occurs so strikingly in *A Thousand-Mile Walk*, presents itself to him again during his residence in Twenty Hill Hollow on the sand of Dry Creek after a washout. "I like to watch the first writings upon the fresh new-made leaflets of Nature's own making," he observed. First came some tracks left by a small mollusc and a blue crane, but Muir quickly skips over these readable recordings to the thought of the palimpsest: "all [the marks] are easily read at present, but soon writing above writing in countless characters will be inscribed on this beautiful sheet, making it yet more beautiful, but also carrying it far beyond our analysis." Just as his first observation on nature's palimpsest led him to a reflection on the unity in diversity of nature, this one leads to another profound extension of the image, this time to the human heart: "In like manner every human heart and mind is written upon as soon as created, and in all lives there are periods of change when by various floods their pages are smoothed like these sand-sheets, preparing them for a series of new impressions, and many an agent is at once set in motion printing and picturing. Happy is the man who is so engraved that when he reaches the calm days of reflection he may rejoice in following the forms of both his upper and under lines" (11). This reflection seems valid in Muir's own case, for this was a period of "calm days of reflection" for him. His own newly cleared soul is not devoid of those memories and images that form the palimpsest of his own soul, no matter how peaceful he may have found his new life in California.

Only a little more than a month after his observation of the *tabula rasa* of Dry Creek, Muir showed once again the influence of his father's harsh fundamentalism upon his own esthetic reaction to nature. Commenting upon the blossoming of flowers after a rain storm, Muir's criticism of the anthropocentric belief in the pre-eminence of "commodity" is couched in an image of reaction to his father: "Parents sometimes lecture children for snipping paper into fanciful shapes. How busily the Creator is at work today upon artificial flower tissue! Those terribly correct parents ought to consider their Creator and learn of Him, or, to be consistent, include Him in their fault-finding lectures forbidding waste of time on frivolous fancy. These grasses and flowers would make as good and as much mutton without such great pains of nicking and printing" (22).

It is also in reaction to his father that Muir discovered a new theme of nature, one that is to become most important in his writing. As Thoreau, in his chapter on "Higher Laws" in *Walden*, tells how "John Farmer" loses sight of the rectilinearity of farm and city, labor and body, through the sound of some flute heard only by himself (the equivalent of Thoreau's own "different drummer"), so Muir is entranced by the sound of "living water" in comparison to his own duties "in full chase of the wretched sheep." His reflection on what appears to him as a mystic revelation is again given entirely in terms of opposition to the doctrine of nature preached by his father: "Everything is governed by laws. I used to imagine that our Sabbath days were recognized by Nature, and that, apart from the moods and feelings in which we learn to move, there was a more or less clearly defined correspondence between the laws of Nature and our own. But out here in the free unplanted fields there is no rectilineal sectioning of times and seasons. All things *flow* here in indivisible, measureless currents" (8). This concept of nature as continual flux is the keynote to a proper understanding of Muir. In a sense, it is the same image as that of the palimpsest, which suggests implicitly that the process of change itself is the greatest beauty in the recording of natural phenomena. As we shall see, this theme becomes most important in his writing.[3]

III *Pastoral Care and Curses*

Muir left no doubt about his opinion of sheep and shepherds in the journal kept at Smoky Jack's camp. Aside from his un-shepherd-like feelings about the rights of coyotes to an occasional feast of mutton, he found little virtue either in the sheep themselves—which he later called "misbegotten . . . semi-manufactured [creatures], made less by God than man" (*My First Summer in the Sierra,* 97)—or in their caretakers, the shepherds. Half humorously, he wondered about the degeneration of the profession, from the "intelligent and lute-voiced" shepherds of Virgil and Milton to the "muddy and degraded" California shepherds. "Milton in his darkness," he concluded, "bewailed the absence of 'flocks and herds,' but I am sure that if all the flocks and herds, together with all the other mongrel victims of civilization, were hidden from me, I should rejoice beyond the possibility of any note of wail" (*John of the Mountains,* 29).

Alas, he was doomed to put up with the depravity of modern pastoral for some time yet. He could escape from Smoky Jack's "felted phalanx" to his beloved Sierra only by agreeing with another shepherd, Patrick Delaney, to assist in the moving of his herd to the mountain pastures of the Sierra during the summer of 1869. Thus the setting for Muir's "first summer in the Sierra" was far from ideal. When he came to write the book in 1911, however, he had become too good a writer not to see the possibilities inherent in the nature of a herd of sheep and some of the crasser specimens of shepherds. The sheep and their shepherds serve admirably in this most artistically successful of Muir's books as a dominant symbol of anti-nature; to it, his own observations of the wild Sierra and of the beauty of nature supply a marvelously effective contrast.

Muir establishes early in the book the opposition of his symbols. Still in the lowlands of the Sierra, near the North Fork of the Merced River, he details the description of a camp made near a grove of incense cedar (*Libocedrus decurrens*): "It would be delightful to be storm-bound beneath one of these noble, hospitable, inviting old trees," he notes, but adds that "the weather is calm tonight, and our camp is only a sheep camp." He then concludes his entry for that day (June 6, 1869) with a lyric burst:

> The night wind is telling the wonders of the upper mountains, their snow fountains and gardens, forests and groves; even their topography is in its tones. And the stars, the everlasting sky lilies, how bright they are now that we have climbed above the lowland dust! The horizon is bounded and adorned by a spiry wall of pines, every tree harmoniously related to every other; definite symbols, divine hieroglyphics written with sunbeams. Would I could understand them! The stream flowing past the camp through ferns and lilies and alders makes sweet music to the ear, but the pines marshaled around the edge of the sky make a yet sweeter music to the eye. Divine beauty all. Here I could stay tethered forever with just bread and water, nor would I be lonely; loved friends and neighbors, as love for everything increased, would seem all the nearer however many the miles and mountains between us. (21-22)

This lovely meditation is then followed by the entry for the following day in sudden and abrupt contrast—"The sheep were sick last night." The contrast continues with a discussion of how the sheep became sick by eating "blessed azalea," which, "'Sheep-men' call . . . 'sheep-poison,' and wonder what the

Creator was thinking about when he made it—so desperately does sheep business blind and degrade" (22).

The contrast continues with a comparison of the shepherds of Scotland and the Middle East with the shepherds of California. The Scottish shepherd loved his work, was "probably descended from a race of shepherds and inherited a love and aptitude for the business almost as marked as that of his collie." The small flocks of the Oriental shepherd allowed him to call each sheep by name and gave him plenty of time for piping, reading, and thinking. But the California shepherd, Muir concluded, "is never quite sane for any considerable time. Of all Nature's voices baa is about all he hears. Even the howls and kiyis of coyotes might be blessings if well heard, but he hears them only through a blur of mutton and wool, and they do him no good" (24).

This comparison continues through the book. Muir leaves the contemplation of a "blessed dell" at the North Fork of the Merced to follow the "hoofed locusts," the "Gadarene swine," along their dusty trail (86). He remarks their amazing stupidity in the matter of crossing water, and ends one detailed narration of a crossing with the comment that "A sheep can hardly be called an animal; an entire flock is required to make one foolish individual" (114). Upon finding some which had strayed from the flock, "huddled in a timid, silent bunch," he observes that they were basely human in their actions: "Having escaped restraint, they were, like some people we know of, afraid of their freedom, did not know what to do with it, and seemed glad to get back into the old familiar bondage" (57).

The sheep are not to blame for their degraded condition. Muir everywhere shows admiration for wild sheep. It is man who has converted the natural beauty of their wildness to a bastard creation that partakes only of the evil of his commercialism. When he observes the flock feeding on a field of lilies, Muir complains sadly not of the sheep themselves, but of man's influence upon them: "And so the beauty of lilies falls on angels and men, bears and squirrels, wolves and sheep, birds and bees, but as far as I have seen, man alone, and the animals he tames, destroy these gardens" (95).

No, the sheep are useful as an ordering symbol of the depradations of man in nature, but punning on their nature and their occupation, Muir holds out his deepest scorn for the "sheepmen" who refuse to see the beauties of nature in any but a commercial mode. "Shepherd Billy," who accompanied him with Delaney's flock through most of the period described in *My First Summer in the Sierra*, comes in for most of the abuse. Muir's description of Billy's untidy appearance is one of the most humorous passages in his writings:

> Following the sheep he carries a heavy six-shooter swung from his belt on one side and his luncheon on the other. The ancient cloth in which the meat, fresh from the frying pan, is tied serves as a filter through which the clear fat and gravy juices drip down on his right hip and leg in clustering stalactites. This oleaginous formation is soon broken up, however, and diffused and rubbed evenly into his scanty apparel, by sitting down, rolling over, crossing his legs while resting on logs, etc., making shirt and trousers water-tight and shiny. His trousers, in particular, have become so adhesive with the mixed fat and resin that pine needles, thin flakes and fibres of bark, hair, mica scales and minute grains of quartz, horneblende, etc., feathers, seed wings, moth and butterfly wings, legs and antennae of innumerable insects, or even whole insects . . . with flower petals, pollen dust and indeed bits of all plants, animals, and minerals of the region adhere to them and are sagely imbedded, so that though far from being a naturalist he collects fragmentary specimens of everything and becomes richer than he knows. His specimens are kept passably fresh, too, by the purity of the air and the resiny bituminous beds into which they are pressed. Man is a microcosm, at least our shepherd is, or rather his trousers. These precious overalls are never taken off, and nobody knows how old they are, though one may guess by their thickness and concentric structure. Instead of wearing thin they wear thick, and in their stratification have no small geological significance.
>
> (129-30)

This extravagant geological and botanical comparison might be considered only good Western humor, if Muir did not notice, as he often does, how strange it is that "mankind alone is dirty" (58), that the mole and the earthworm, and even the squirrel, who spends so much of his lifetime in resinous matter, seem always to be *clean* in nature, while man alone is dirtied by his occupation. The moral must seem so obvious to Muir that he never makes it explicit.

To Muir Billy's physical uncleanliness is as nothing compared to his spiritual condition. Muir reports in direct quotation many examples of Billy and the other shepherds' unwillingness to see

the beauty of nature; apparently he quotes them in an effort
to make what seems incredible to him believable to his readers.
After marveling over the size and beauty of a growth of *Pteris
aquilina,* some of which were over seven feet tall, Muir has this
conversation with a passing shepherd:

> "What do you think of these grand ferns?" I asked.
> "Oh, they're only d-----d big brakes," he replied.   (41)

When he tries to get Billy to look at Yosemite, Billy's only
reply is "What is Yosemite but . . . a lot of rocks—a hole in the
ground—a place dangerous about falling into—a d-----d good
place to keep away from" (147).

Opposed to the spiritual uncleanliness of the sheep and shepherds Muir places a wild inhabitant of the Sierra, the bear. The
natural dignity of these animals leads him to report a narrative
in which a bear shows up rather well in comparison with himself. Such an occasion is rather rare in Muir's writing, although
he was probably delighted to be able to picture himself in
something less than a heroic posture. Observing a bear from
a hidden place, Muir decided he would like to see the animal
run; so he rushed at him, fully expecting to observe him
running away. To his dismay, the bear "stood his ground ready
to fight and defend himself," and Muir feared that it would be
he who would do the running. The "strenuous interview" lasted
until the bear, with dignity intact, "in the slow fullness of time
. . . pulled his huge paws down off the log, and with magnificent
deliberation turned and walked leisurely up the meadow . . .
evidently neither fearing me very much nor trusting me" (137).

As we might expect, lesser men fare less well with the same
creature. When the other shepherds encounter bears, they have
no dignity at all. They are quickly put to rout up trees or onto
roofs by the hungry bears, and are derided by Muir for their
lack of bravery (they of course have guns; he had none)
(209ff). In the contrast between bears and men in this book
the only character who seems to have Muir's approval is David
Brown, a famous bear hunter. Muir recounts at length and with
great respect Brown's technique for hunting bear. Brown has an
equal respect for the bears as worthy opponents to his skill.
Indeed, Brown shares Muir's feelings about the bears' rights
to turnabout, to biting the biter. Muir quotes him as saying
that, "if an old lean hungry mother with cubs met a man on her
own ground she would," in Brown's opinion, "try to catch and

eat him. This would be only fair play anyhow, for we eat them" (30). Judging from the respect Muir shows for Brown's opinions, Muir's feelings about hunting are very like those of Thoreau, Chaucer, and Faulkner. Though he would not hunt himself, he did feel that, if the proprieties were upheld, if the animals were hunted with a proper decorum, and if they were allowed to exercise their native dignity, then, like Chaucer's monk he would "yaf not of that text a pulled hen/That saith that hunters ben not hooly men."

Halfway between the bears, the other wild creatures, and the degeneracy of the shepherds are the Indians. Muir's attitude toward California Indians is mixed. He has respect for their capacity to live with nature, to be free of the bonds of civilized customs and "necessities," and for their native capacity for stealth and for endurance. He seems to find them more comparable with the wild animals than with men (not, of course, in Muir's lexicon an invidious comparison at all), but in the matter of cleanliness they stand up badly against the animals. He is most severe toward them when they show signs of bad judgment to him—a preference for the vices of civilization to the virtues of natural living. When he is stopped by a band of Indians in Bloody Canyon and begged for whiskey and tobacco, his repulsion is apparent, but it not at all self-assured. He noted his reaction: "How glad I was to get away from the gray grim crowd and see them vanish down the trail! Yet it seems sad to feel such desperate repulsion from one's fellow beings, however degraded. To prefer the society of squirrels and woodchucks to that of our own species must surely be unnatural" (219).

The Indians are not much to be preferred over the final class of human creatures described in *My First Summer in the Sierra,* the tourists. Even these, though they frighten the birds and squirrels with their "glaring tailored" clothes and "seem to care but little for the glorious objects about them," are not all bad. Once they "are fairly within the mighty walls of the temple [of Yosemite] and hear the falls, they will forget themselves and become devout" (104). Muir is no snob about "his" wild nature. He is willing to share it with all; indeed, he is eager that even the most hopelessly unregenerate victim of civilization allow himself the opportunity to "become devout" in the temple of nature. Else, why these many books? Muir is in this book, as everywhere, a proselytizer for his own worship; he believes strongly that all may profit from the experiences he describes.

IV *The Call of the Wild*

From the catalog just given of the *dramatis personae* of Muir's first summer in the Sierra, I have tried to suggest that in this book Muir has succeeded in developing a thematic polarity between the dignity of wild creatures and the degeneracy of the tame. I believe this to be his most successful book, the one that new readers of Muir might best start with because of its thematic success and because of the delicate balance kept between the narrative of these other characters and the pure description and sensibility of Muir himself. There is a great deal of description in this book, as in all of Muir's writing; and there are also many more "characters" taking part than those described above. Some of Muir's best descriptions of insects appear here: the "small savage black ant," which, Muir believes, might be called "the master existence of this vast mountain world" (43); the ubiquitous housefly and the jolly grasshopper (138-39); mosquitoes, borers, and gall-flies (169-70) all have a part in the mountain life he describes.

Here also are his first observations of the water ouzel, which becomes almost the hero of *The Mountains of California*. His description of the bird in this book is in some ways more charming than the more definitive later ones.[4] In sum, this book has all of the best of Muir: a thematic and meaningful development of the opposition of nature and culture; fresh, unsophisticated observations of both the ordinary and the extraordinary; and enough lyric and transcendent passages to make the narrative much more than a mere travelogue. It is also a key volume in his life. *The Mountains of California, Steep Trails,* and all the other later Muir works represent a man *committed* to the wilderness life; this book, like *A Thousand-Mile Walk,* represents Muir *in the process of becoming* committed, and is thus even more interesting in terms of Muir's psychology.

The call of the wild is the more attractive to Muir in contrast to the burden of the sheep. He speaks nowhere in a more pathetic voice than at the end of this volume when, the season closing, the flock must return to the lowlands:

> If I had a few sacks of flour, an axe and some matches, I would build a cabin of pine logs, pile up plenty of firewood about it and stay all winter to see the grand fertile snow-storms, watch the birds and animals that winter thus high, how they

live, how the forests look snow-laden or buried, and how the avalanches look and sound on their way down the mountains. But now I'll have to go, for there is nothing to spare in the way of provisions. I'll surely be back, however, surely I'll be back. No other place has ever so overwhelmingly attracted me as this hospitable, Godful wilderness. (241)

Thoreau could borrow an axe; but Patrick Delaney was not to play Emerson to Muir, at least not to that extent.

One question must be asked. What was there, in this first summer spent in the Sierra, that could produce this reaction in Muir, that could change the general desire to escape civilization apparent at the end of his one-thousand mile walk to a specific desire to remain, as he did, for no less than nine years in and among the mountains of California? The answer, on many levels, is given in this volume.

In the first place, wild nature is most completely identified with the mountains. Muir specifically compares the permanence of the mountains with the lowlands. Tracks and trails in the mountains are like "light ornamental stitching or embroidering," but in the lowlands the white man blasts roads out of solid rock, dams and "tames" streams "to work in mines like slaves" and to riddle and strip the face of the earth for his convenience (55). Man gives the name of the devil to aspects of the mountains in place names like "Devil's Slide," but Muir is sure that the devil is a lowland dweller—"his tracks are seldom seen above the timber line" (150).

Second, part of the Transcendental canon is the notion that the greatest unity can be found through contemplation and absorption of the greatest diversity. The mountains of California represent such a diversity to Muir. The Sierra becomes to him a microcosm. Looking up Bloody Canyon from the valley, he is struck by the diversity of vegetation and climate available within a few miles: "The lilies on the bank of Moraine Lake are higher than my head, and the sunshine is hot enough for palms. Yet the snow round the arctic gardens at the summit of the pass is plainly visible, only about four miles away, and between lie specimen zones of all the principal climates of the globe. In little more than an hour one may swoop down from winter to summer, from an arctic to a torrid region, through as great changes of climate as one would encounter in traveling from Labrador to Florida" (225).

And third there is something essentially holy and awe-inspiring in the sublimity of mountains. "No Sierra landscape" that he has ever seen "holds anything truly dead or dull. . . . Everything is perfectly clean and pure and full of divine lessons." Mountains invoke in Muir Emerson's concept of metaphor as more descriptive of reality than the language of exact reporting; the height of mountains heightens his response to them: "When we try to pick out anything by itself, we find it hitched to everything else in the universe. One fancies a heart like our own must be beating in every crystal and cell, and we feel like stopping to speak to the plants and animals as friendly fellow mountaineers. Nature as a poet, an enthusiastic workingman, becomes more and more visible the farther and higher we go; for the mountains are fountains—beginning places, however related to sources beyond mortal ken" (157-58).

In his beloved mountains, Muir becomes, like Emerson, a transparent eyeball, open, passive to the wonders of nature surrounding him. This religious and mystic sensation occurs to him immediately upon arriving at the foothills of the Sierra— "We are now in the mountains and they are in us, kindling enthusiasm, making every nerve quiver, filling every pore and cell of us. Our flesh-and-bone tabernacle seems transparent as glass to the beauty about us, as if truly an inseparable part of it, thrilling with the air and trees, streams and rocks, in the waves of the sun,—a part of all nature, neither old nor young, sick nor well, but immortal" (16). With these sensations, the wonder is that he could ever return to the lowlands.

Indeed, his reporting of experience in this book has a heightened perception not evident in either *The Story of My Boyhood and Youth* or *A Thousand-Mile Walk*. Even an apparently simple experience—sleeping one night on a square-cut boulder in the Merced River—is transformed into a mystic communion:

> When I climbed on top of [the boulder] today and lay down to rest, it seemed the most romantic spot I had yet found. . . . How soothingly, restfully cool it is beneath that leafy, translucent ceiling, and how delightful the water music—the deep bass tones of the fall, the clashing ringing spray, and infinite variety of small low tones of the current gliding past the side of the boulder-island. . . . All this shut in; every one of these influences acting at short range as if in a quiet room. The place seemed holy, where one might hope to see God.

> After dark, when the camp was at rest, I groped my way back to the altar boulder and passed the night on it,—above the water, beneath the leaves and the stars,—everything still more impressive than by day, the fall seen dimly white, singing Nature's old love song with solemn enthusiasm, while the stars peering through the leaf-roof seemed to join in the white water's song. Precious night, precious day to abide in me forever. Thanks be to God for his immortal gift. (48-49)

When the experience becomes yet more sublime, when danger is added to delight, the pitch of experience and expression becomes correspondingly more intense. Muir's first view of Yosemite Falls was from the top of a ridge, from hard-purchased hand and foot-holds along the Mono Trail side of the cliff up to Yosemite Creek. From that point he moved along even more precarious holds to a ridge right over the stream—a several thousand-foot drop. "The swift-roaring flood beneath, overhead, and beside me was very nerve-trying. I therefore concluded not to venture further but did nevertheless." Chewing tufts of bitter artemisia to prevent giddiness, he struggled to a tiny ledge "close to the outplunging current" and remained there, "not distinctly conscious of danger," depending upon his body to take "keen care for safety on its own account" for he knew not how long a period. The enjoyment he noted upon his return to camp was "enough to kill if that were possible" (118-20). His dreams in the camp that evening were of mountains collapsing beneath his feet, so realistic that he woke up at one point, crying out, "This time it is real—all must die, and where could mountaineer find a more glorious death!" (121).

Sublimity would not be sublime if it occurred too frequently, and such narrations as the preceding are rare in Muir. The pace of his observations is more commonly smooth and, to use an image that is common in this volume, flowing. It is the constant flow of nature that is most striking to Muir and most beautifully described in his works. I pointed out earlier in this chapter that Muir first develops the theme of flux in nature during the winter preceding this first summer in the Sierra. In *My First Summer* it is almost omnipresent as a theme. Flowing clouds and streams, the continual building up and wearing away of the mountains themselves, all these phenomena seem to Muir to be constant proof of the eternal presence of God in nature. One of his most lyric passages in this book traces the natural history of a drop of rain as it passes through the mountains (125-27). Another is an extension of the concept of flux to the entire universe:

> Contemplating the lace-like fabric of streams outspread over the mountains, we are reminded that everything is flowing— going somewhere, animals and so-called lifeless rocks as well as water. Thus the snow flows fast or slow in grand beauty-making glaciers and avalanches; the air in majestic floods carrying minerals, plant leaves, seeds, spores, with streams of music and fragrance; water streams carrying rocks both in solution and in form of mud particles, sand, pebbles, and boulders. Rocks flow from volcanoes like water from springs, and animals flock together and flow in currents modified by stepping, leaping, gliding, flying, swimming, etc. While the stars go streaming through space pulsed on and on forever like blood globules in Nature's warm heart. (236)

The ebb and flow of natural processes, the polarity of wild nature and the depravity of man, the process of Muir's own increasing involvement with the wilderness in general and with the Sierra Nevada and the valley of the Yosemite in particular combine through the catalyst of Muir's first summer in the Sierra to make this his most rewarding book. Published late in his life, it has advantages of both youth and age: the freshness of his youthful vision upon a new scene, the careful artistry in revision of his journal for publication by a man who had, in 1911, spent most of his last forty years in the wilderness and had written many volumes about his experiences. Though precisely that combination of fortuitous circumstances does not occur again in Muir's writings, we shall see that *My First Summer in the Sierra* is only the best of many very good books about Muir's life in Western wildernesses.

CHAPTER 4

Mountains of Ice, Mountains of Rock

I *The Transcendental Paradox*

NO STUDENT of American writing in the Transcendental vein can avoid a certain wonder at the bulk of published work of writers like Muir, Emerson, and Thoreau. Their collected works contrast in size strangely with their published opinions about the relative virtue of writing and comprehending. Emerson lashed out at the retrospective tendencies of an age which wrote, "biographies, histories, and criticism," and then . . . wrote biographies, histories, and criticism. Thoreau complained that though much is published, little is printed; and then . . . had *A Week on the Concord and Merrimack Rivers* published. And Muir remarked in his journal that, "instead of narrowing my attention to bookmaking out of material already eaten and drunken, I would rather stand in what all the world would call an idle manner, literally gaping with all the mouths of soul and body, demanding nothing, fearing nothing, but hoping and enjoying enormously. So called sentimental, transcendental dreaming seems the only sensible and substantial business that one can engage in" (*John of the Mountains,* 102). And then . . . rushed to print.

The unsympathetic reader is inclined to believe such statements to be part of a pose, that Transcendental writers were as eager to publish their writings as the lowliest hack. More intelligent critics, incorrectly I believe, dismiss the paradox by assuming that the Transcendentalist attains a kind of amateur standing as a writer while remaining a professional at some other occupation—Emerson as an eclectic idealist philosopher, Thoreau as a theorist on the art of living, Muir as a mountaineer and guide. Neither point of view does justice to any of these men. A careful study of their works must lead to the conclusion that each was a thorough professional as a writer; that an infinity of care, far exceeding that of the writer of fiction, went into all of their works; that, indeed, they can only be compared with poets so far as their use of language is concerned. Emerson developed, in the "Language" section of *Nature*, a whole *Poetics* of the use of metaphor as an agent of Transcendental description. Thoreau's rhetoric is charged with two and three-level puns, ironies, and allegories—all intended to convey meaning beyond superficial description. And Muir, despairing at first, eventually became almost as adept as his two great predecessors at the poet's task of suggesting through the emotions infinitely more than he seems to be saying to the intellect.

It is true that Muir came late to writing. His first book was not published until he was fifty-six, his first magazine article when he was thirty-four. Moreover, his beginning thoughts about language and nature were the opposite of Emerson's, a disadvantage which required years for him to overcome. Emerson believed that words were "noble races of creatures . . . profusions of forms . . . hosts of orbs in heaven," which were debased to serve as a "grammar of [man's] municipal speech." He believed that "a fact is the end or last issue of spirit," and therefore that language was best and most naturally used as descriptive metaphor of conditions in nature through which the spirit of God was made manifest. Muir believed, contrarily, that natural phenomena speak for themselves and that any attempt to reproduce their voices must necessarily be something of a misrepresentation. His best statement on the subject is a consideration of the Merced River, which he believed to be unequaled in its capacity to speak to man about the beauty of nature:

> Thousands of joyous streams are born in the snowy range, but not a poet among them all can sing like the Merced. Men are not born equal, neither are rivers. The Merced was born a poet, a perfect seraph among its fellows. The first utterances of its childhood are sweet, uncommon song, and in its glorious harmonies of manhood it excells all the vocal waters of the world, and when its days of mountain sublimity are past, in quiet age down on the plain amid land-waves of purple and gold, its lifeblood throbs with poetic emotion, and with a smooth sheet of soft music it hushes and tinkles and goes to its death in a maze of dripping willows and broad green oaks—an Amazon of thoughtfulness and majesty. Ah, who shall describe these golden plains of age, these grand green forests of spruce and boundless tangles

of blooming shrubs, and the level velvet glacial daisy-gentian meadows in which the gleaming arteries of this most noble of rivers lie? *(John of the Mountains, 57)*

The very creation of this metaphor—river as poet—argues a high poetic talent in Muir. Still, what the metaphor says *literally* about the Merced River and, by extension, what it suggests about Muir's opinion of the voice of all natural phenomena become a limiting factor in his writing. Not only are words inadequate to speak in comparison to the nobler language of the phenomena of nature themselves, but all art is helpless, according to Muir, in comparison with the thing described. Sketching on the North Dome in Yosemite, Muir "would fain draw everything in sight—rock, tree, and leaf. But little can I do beyond mere outlines,—marks with meanings like words, readable only to myself." Though he persevered in this instance, he had little real hope of being able to communicate through his sketches: "Whether these picture-sheets are to vanish like fallen leaves or go to friends like letters matters not much; for little can they tell to those who have not themselves seen similar wildness, and like a language have learned it" (*My First Summer,* 131). For Muir, at least at this stage of his life, art and artifice are not to be trusted; experience and memory of experience are the only possible grounds of communication. And even experience of nature is not enough. Nature must be learned, like a new language, by communion with it. Small wonder that he waited so long before attempting what he considered at first as a futile and meaningless experiment.

II *Mountains of Ice*

Having these feelings about the impossibility of communicating the real spirit of nature, Muir was naturally unwilling to narrow his "attention to bookmaking." Instead, he was dragged into authorship by the very intensity of his beliefs about the beauty of the orderly processes of nature. After descending with Pat Delaney's flock to the lowlands in the fall of 1869, he returned to Yosemite to seek casual employment and to be near his beloved "range of light," as he believed the Sierra Nevada (range of snow) should have been named. Ostensibly employed to run a sawmill, he spent much of his time guiding parties of tourists through the Yosemite, and he came in frequent contact with *The Yosemite Guide Book,* which had been written by Josiah D. Whitney, Professor of Geology at Harvard and State Geologist of California. It was in reaction to Whitney's belief that the Yosemite had been formed by cataclysmic geological processes that Muir became, almost in spite of himself, a writer.

Muir was not a scientist, his scientific training at the University of Wisconsin notwithstanding. Or, if he was a scientist, he was never *only* a scientist. A scientist examines phenomena with as much objectivity as possible and attempts to account for them. Muir developed a philosophical concept of nature from a very limited view of nature, conditioned by a predisposition toward idealism, and then he fit his observations into the frame of that concept. That is not to say that the results of his observations were not often scientifically accurate, but to a true scientist method is all in all. In his controversy with Professor Whitney, Muir was, as it happened, more nearly correct than his learned opponent. However, Muir's biographers have done both men a disservice by exaggerating the scientific nature of Muir's position in the controversy. By not recognizing the philosophical and moral conditions which were responsible for what are essentially scientificating rationalizations on Muir's part, critics have been fair neither to Muir nor to Whitney.

By the time his first summer in the Sierra had come to an end, the doctrine of the eternal flux of nature was fixed permanently in Muir's mind. The concept apparently occurred to him for the first time in Cuba, when he dismissed the idea that the agave made "a mighty effort to flower and mature its seeds and then to die of exhaustion" with the comment that "there is not . . . a mighty effort or the need of one in wild nature. She accomplishes her ends without unquiet effort" (*A Thousand-Mile Walk,* 378). His observations in California only served to confirm his belief. To have someone suggest that the most beautiful of the valleys of the Sierra was the result of "a mighty effort," and not the result of a process of gradual change, was to challenge not merely Muir's scientific observations but his whole philosophical *raison d'être.*

Whitney believed that the valley of the Yosemite had been formed at the time of the faulting which produced the Sierra Nevada. As he put it, "there was at the Yosemite a subsidence of a limited area, marked by lines of 'fault' or fissures" and that, in fact, "the bottom of the valley sank down to an unknown

depth, owing to its support being withdrawn from underneath."[1]
Muir simply refused to believe that the most beautiful of the
wilderness phenomena which he had yet encountered and to
which he had dedicated his life could be the result of an action
which appeared contrary to all of his observations about the
spirit of nature. The lines were drawn; the battle was engaged.
It was a battle in which Muir's only weapon was his pen. He
began to write.

There was nothing scientific about his desire to contradict
Whitney. His journal entries for this period show a militant de-
termination, an almost religious fervor: "I will brood above the
Merced Mountains like a cloud until all the ice rivers of this
mighty system are fully restored, each in its channel, harmonious
as a song. . . . Heaven knows that John the Baptist was not
more eager to get all his fellow sinners into the Jordan than I
to baptize all of mine in the beauty of God's mountains" (*John
of the Mountains*, 86). Evidence of glacial action was only a
tool for Muir's purpose of restoring harmony to the vision of
the Yosemite, to reveal that "the beauty of God's mountains"
was the result of an orderly process.

His first effort in the controversy (and his first published
writing, if we exclude an apocryphal anonymous contribution
to the Boston *Recorder* of 1864) was a letter to the New York
Tribune, dated from Yosemite on September 28 and published
on December 5, 1871. It is a remarkable production, both for
its content and its style, reminiscent of the scientific writings of
renaissance baroque. The central portion, of about two-thousand
words, is an attempt to reconstruct the flow, appearance, and
history of the glaciers which formed the valley of the Yosemite
and adjacent valleys in the Sierra. That part is written in lucid,
workmanlike, scientific prose. Framing this narrative, however,
are two of the most poetic passages Muir ever wrote, one successful, the other ludicrous. The tailpiece is a lovely evocation of
the continuity of the processes of nature through the image of
Muir's own campfire. The headpiece is a self-conscious, man-
nered attempt to apply a variation of one of Muir's favorite
images, the palimpsest, to the situation of the glaciers of
Yosemite. Muir was fortunate that there was in 1871 no flippant
New Yorker editor to caution him to "block that metaphor" in
the opening passage:

> Two years ago, when picking flowers in the mountains back of
> Yosemite valley, I found a book. It was blotted and storm-beaten;

all of its outer pages were mealy and crumbly, the paper seemed to dissolve like the snow beneath which it had been buried; but many of the inner pages had been preserved, and though all were more or less stained and torn, whole chapters were easily readable. In just this condition is the great open book of Yosemite glaciers today; its granite pages have been torn and blurred by the same storms that wasted the castaway book. The grand central chapters of the Hoffman and Tenaya and Nevada glaciers are stained and corroded by the frosts and rains, yet, nevertheless, they contain scarce one unreadable page, but the outer chapters of the . . . Yosemite . . . are all dimmed and eaten away on the bottom, though the tops of their pages have not been so long exposed, and still proclaim, in splendid characters the glorious action of their departed ice.

This trumped-up comparison is the more disgraced in contrast with the validity of the image used to end his essay, an asseveration of the unity of the flow of nature drawn from the energy cycle of plants:

> I have set fire to two pine logs, and the neighboring trees are coming to my charmed circle of light. . . . Grandly do my logs give back their light, slow gleaned from suns of a hundred summers, garnered beautifully away in dotted cells and in beads of amber gum; and together with this outgush of light, seems to flow all the other riches of their life, and their living companions are looking down as if to witness their perfect and beautiful death.[2]

One might speculate that Muir learned from the failure of the introductory passage that in scientific writing, at least, one need not seem to apologize for the evidence marshaled to support one's case. In the series of articles published in *The Overland Monthly* about the Yosemite glaciers he is more careful about extended metaphors, though in one, "Ancient Glaciers and Their Pathways," he cannot resist the temptation to refer briefly to the "hieroglyphics" that are engraved, "line upon line," over the rocks.[3]

As a rule, these articles are quite rigid in their scientific documentation and vocabulary, but in final summary paragraphs Muir permits himself to expatiate a bit on the deeper meanings of the evidence of flow, slow change, and their relationship to the beauty of the mountains. At the conclusion of the article "Mountain Sculpture," he noted that, mighty as the effect of the glaciers appears to us to have been on the rocks, "it has only developed the predestined forms of mountain beauty which were ready and waiting to receive the baptism of light" (16). Concluding the essay on the continuity of the origin of the Yosemite, he pointed out the unity of processes going on in all the Sierra valleys at once (31). And, at the end of the article entitled "Ancient Glaciers," he delighted in observing that what appeared magnificent to man is really only an understatement to the omnipotence of nature: "When we walk the pathways of Yosemite glaciers and contemplate their separate works—the mountains they have shaped, the canyons they have furrowed, the rocks they have worn, and broken, and scattered in moraines —on reaching Yosemite, instead of being overwhelmed as at first with its uncompared magnitude, we ask, *Is this all?* wondering that so mighty a concentration of energy did not find yet grander expression" (47).

Modern geologists agree that Muir "won" his disagreement with Whitney. His reading of the evidence was closer to the truth than Whitney's, although modern techniques have shown that Muir was not entirely correct in assuming that all of the processes involved at Yosemite were non-cataclysmic. For the present study the only importance of the controversy was its single great effect upon Muir—it compelled him to ignore his own beliefs about the inadequacy of language to describe nature. It drove him to convince others of the validity of at least one aspect of his own experience in the Sierra wilderness. That these first communications were virtually devoid of literary interest is less important than the fact that he had made a start. An idea which he held about a natural process had been communicated successfully to others. He may have begun to feel after these limited successes the possibility of communicating something even *more* important about the spiritual beauty of nature. Thus one naturalist became a writer.

III *Emerson*

But Muir was not a writer yet. The language of scientific description, with its concomitant graphs and sketches, is a far cry from the prose of which Muir was capable. Though he managed to raise the level of his purely scientific writings about Sierra glaciers nearly to the status of literature, he did so at the expense of making those essays less effective as scientific documents. He was still in the first stages of experimentation with his new talent, and, between 1871 and 1874, he might have gone in any number of directions with his writing.

His journals of these years are particularly interesting for the evidence they give of his willingness to experiment in different forms. Unsure of himself, he attempted things which he had not tried since his woefully unsuccessful beginnings in his Madison years. One can imagine the frustrations he must have felt at this time, frustrations which were strong enough to drive him to primitivism in verse:

> The Valley is tranquil and sunful
> And Winter delayeth his coming.
> The river sleeps currentless in deep mirror pools,
> The falls scarce whisper.
> The brown meadows bask,
> The domes bathe dreamily in deep azure sky,
> And all the day is Light.   (*John of the Mountains,* 91)

Muir sensed that the experience he wished to communicate, beyond his need for the specific acceptance of the glacial theory, was essentially an emotional one and was fit matter for poetry. But his attempts in that direction were invariably unsuccessful, and it is not difficult to see why.

Primitive verses like the one quoted above were simply not suited to the feeling Muir had about the wild nature he loved. The necessity to condense, to compress his feelings into anything as "regular" as the first two lines of the quoted verse was quite contrary to what he felt the subject demanded. This little bit of verse, in fact, is quite a revealing document concerning Muir's capabilities for poetry. As the landscape opens before him, the mechanics of poetry dissolve in Muir's desire to express as perfectly as possible his sensation. This example is almost unique in his journals; he must have felt that there were no possibilities in that direction.

What of the other direction, though, toward freedom in expansive verse, *à la* Whitman? Muir has also left one example of an experiment in that technique in his journals. Under the notation, "looking up from the foot of the First fall at the bottom of the gorge between Upper and Lower Yosemite Falls," appears this passage: "Terrible energy, roar and surge, flapping, dashing, storm-sustained exultant power! Glorious maelstrom of irised foam taking forms and movements of flame—a halo of beauty encompassing the wild uproar night and day . . ." (*John of the Mountains,* 128). Fortunately, Muir's sense of self-criticism was good enough to make him recognize that such writing emphasized his worst qualities out of all proportion, while it did not communicate what he felt was most important in descriptions of nature—the recognition of orderly and therefore beautiful processes. Muir's worst fault as a writer was his love for the adjective and, in particular, for the adjective "glorious." This epithetic free verse pandered to that fault and was obviously a dead end. Again, this is the only example of so purple a passage in his journals.

A more fertile path toward development as a writer was reinforced in May of 1871 when Ralph Waldo Emerson arrived in Yosemite and, with a band of unfortunately genteel Eastern companions, spent several days with Muir admiring the grandeur of the Sierra. Although the experience was not entirely a transcendent success,[4] direct contact with the one man Muir might honestly call "master" ought not to be undervalued. Certainly his journals for this period and shortly afterward have a sudden increase in entries of which the following are typical:

> Nature, while urging to utmost efforts, leading us with work, presenting cause beyond cause in endless chains, lost in infinite distances, yet cheers us like a mother with tender prattle words of love, ministering to all our friendliness and weariness.

> The astronomer looks high, the geologist low. Who looks between on the surface of the earth? The farmer, I suppose, but too often he sees only grain, and of that only the mere bread-bushel-and-price side of it.   (*John of the Mountains,* 66-67)

Emerson's influence on Muir is everywhere apparent, but entries like these, coming at about the same time as Emerson's visit, suggest that the visit served to recharge Muir's Transcendental battery, as it were, and to give him new faith in a course of life to which he had already committed himself and to suggest a mode of expression. But, alas the Transcendental paradox! Emerson was unquestionably no less the direct influence upon thoughts more specifically related to Muir's problem of communication:

> I have a low opinion of books; they are but piles of stones set up to show coming travellers where other minds have been, or at best signal smokes to call attention. Cadmus and all the

other inventors of letters receive a thousand-fold more credit than they deserve. *No amount of word-making will ever make a single soul to know these mountains.* [Italics mine.] As well seek to warm the naked and frostbitten by lectures on caloric and pictures of flame. [Compare *Richard II,* I, iii, 294-302.] One day's exposure to mountains is better than cartloads of books. See how willingly Nature poses herself upon photographers' plates. No earthy chemicals are so sensitive as those of the human soul. All that is required is exposure, and purity of material. 'The pure in heart shall see God!'

(John of the Mountains, 94-95)

Again, we are at a dead end. Despite all the specifically literary tugging and hauling of Emerson and Thoreau upon him, Muir was never to write a *Nature* or a *Walden.* Though he filled his writings with Transcendental descriptions, many of them at considerable length, he always required a more specific reason to begin to write. In one case, it was to restore to the common view of his most beloved wilderness the flow of mountains of ice. In another it was to retain for man the possibility of seeing, untrammeled, the great mountains of rock.

IV *The National Parks*

Except for his glacier articles in *The Overland Monthly* and entries in his journals, Muir did little writing until 1875, when he came down from the Sierra, his controversy with Whitney over the glacial origin of Yosemite won, to take up a new battle. He could not bring himself to write books to act as "signal smokes" for Yosemite tourists, but the preservation of the mountain wilderness against the forces of what Emerson had called "commodity" was another matter. Muir was in a fine position during the years before 1875 to observe the inroads being made upon the natural beauty of the Sierra, first by the "hoofed locusts"—herds of sheep like the one he had himself assisted in 1869—and then by cattle growers and farmers. What, after all, was the point of worrying about writing of the deeper meaning of an experience in nature if the physical basis for the experience is destroyed? A new order of necessity had presented itself, and Muir rose to the occasion.

The best strategy to counteract the destruction of the beauty of the Sierra was clear by 1875. Muir's scientific opponent in the glacier matter, Josiah Whitney, had himself pioneered the principal counterattack. In 1866 he had pushed a bill through the California legislature to preserve, by a grant from the federal government, "for public use, resort and recreation," the Mariposa Big Tree Grove and the valley of the Yosemite. And the federal government itself had established in 1872 the first National Park at Yellowstone. The means was established. The only problem remaining to Muir was to convince the people of the United States and their elected representatives that the wilderness, his wilderness, needed to be protected. Muir became a publicist, a one-man Madison Avenue of the transcendent beauty of the wilderness.

He started his crusade in a small way, but it built up quickly. On January 25, 1875, he accepted an invitation to lecture at the Literary Institute of Sacramento. Terrified to the point of nausea, he nevertheless overcame his fear so well that the newspaper account of his first lecture pronounced him to be "at once the most unartistic and refreshing, the most unconventional and positive lecturer we have yet had in Sacramento."[5] Though he never entirely overcame his nervous apprehension, he continued to lecture on the subject of conservation for the remainder of his life.

Newspapers, of course, offered another fertile field for publicity. On February 5, 1875, the Sacramento *Record-Union* carried his first article on conservation. Urging that the state take over the problem of forestation in California, the article is largely practical and pragmatic in its approach. Muir pointed out the shortsightedness of *laissez-faire* exploitation of a natural resource which, in terms of water supply alone, is far more valuable in the long run than any current gain from timbering profits. Other articles, less specifically directed to the California legislature followed in the San Francisco *Bulletin* through 1877. Gradually, these articles became less pragmatic in tone and more of a platform for Muir's views on the esthetic virtues of the preservation of natural beauties.

But both of these media were too limited in their circulation to allow Muir much success in what he knew must be a mass movement of public opinion in America. Even *The Overland Monthly,* which published articles by Muir as early as 1872 and was a satisfactory periodical for the glacier controversy, had a limited national circulation. To touch the American public in general, Muir knew he would have to reach across the continent to New York, where the only truly national magazines in America, *Harper's Monthly* and *Scribner's Monthly* (which became, in 1881, *The Century Magazine*), were published.

His aspiration, though motivated by sentiments far purer than those of the average American writer, was shared by thousands. The great New York magazines a decade after the Civil War had become an immense force in American culture and, indeed, in the development of American literature. With circulations around the 100,000 mark (*The Century* was to exceed 250,000 within the next decade), these periodicals, giants for their time, carried enormous prestige and not a little money to those fortunate enough to have writings printed on their pages. Furthermore, though *Harper's* was known to favor English writings somewhat, both had reputations as *national* magazines, in terms of both their contributors and their circulation. If Muir could have an article accepted by either one of these magazines, the prospects for conservation would become appreciably brighter.

I must admit that at this point I am forced to speculate on matters which are simply not provable, but Muir's first contribution to *Harper's Magazine*, "Living Glaciers of California," published in the November, 1875, issue, seems to bear all the hallmarks of an essay written with the express purpose of "getting into *Harper's*." If he did take the trouble to look up the contents of a few back issues, he would have found that the magazine favored articles on the exotic (glaciers are exotic), on American subjects (these glaciers are in California), written by an expert (Muir's glacier studies in *The Overland Monthly* qualified him as an expert), with a high informational content (the article is purely informational), and that could be easily illustrated with steel engravings (mountains and snow are ideal). Once this essay, a supremely ordinary one, had been published, Muir might reasonably expect that those Eastern editors would smile favorably on less ordinary contributions. He was exactly right.

In 1877 he contributed two more articles to *Harper's* about exotic American phenomena slightly removed from glaciation, but about which he might still be presumed to be an expert. "Snow-banners of the California Alps" (July) and "Snow-Storm on Mount Shasta" (September, 1877) are among the finest pieces of narrative prose written by Muir,[6] but both are exotic, American, eye-witness accounts of highly informative and illustratable phenomena. John Muir, for the cause of conservation, had become a "formula" writer! And the formula worked, for the editors of *Scribner's Monthly* were so impressed by these articles published by their competitor that they promptly took over as publisher for articles by Muir that were *not* written to *Harper's* formula and that led to Muir's eventual success as a writer and to the preservation of Yosemite National Park.

Scribner's Monthly and its successor, *The Century,* was probably the finest magazine ever published in America. Under the able editorship of Richard Watson Gilder and his associate editor, Robert Underwood Johnson, it set standards of quality for American periodicals from about 1878 until the turn of the century. These standards are still valid. Blessed with a remarkable talent to discover and to honor new talent, the editors were forward-looking in all esthetic and social respects. The magazine led editorial battles for fair housing in New York, civil service reform, international copyright, and, as we shall see, the National Park Service. The magazine pioneered in technique and excellence of illustration. It was the foremost Northern periodical to publish the works of a new generation of Southern writers after the Civil War, and it gloried in contributions from all parts of the United States. Muir could not have placed his writings in better hands than those of its editors.

His nine articles written between 1878 and 1882 for *Scribner's Monthly,* which were *not* written to a formula, supply the nucleus to all of his California books except *My First Summer in the Sierra.* These articles also succeeded in setting before a wider audience than did any of Muir's books a point of view about wild nature that was, ten years after they were published, to bring about the result for which they were originally written. They are, literally, articles that changed—or better, retained— the shape of the land. They are also, both in their periodical form and as they were finally shaped into Muir's books about California, enduring literature.

V *The Mountains of California*

The tasks Muir faced in 1894 while compiling *The Mountains of California* were more editorial than authorial. For that reason, it seems sensible to move out of the chronology of his life to consider this book now. He had little writing to do. He did some pruning here, perhaps added a pertinent anecdote or additional description there, but the production of Muir's first book was primarily a problem of selecting and arranging material already written. He would have preferred, as we have seen in the three of his books considered so far, to arrange the material in a simple chronological order. But the mountains of California and his observations upon them rather defy chronology as a guideline. He determined, then, to organize the book spatially. The volume moves from general to specific, from abstract to concrete, while the personal nature of the narrative is kept apparent by references to Muir himself as observer.

The volume opens with three chapters describing the general aspects of the Sierra Nevada themselves, their glaciers, and their snow fields. These most salient aspects of the mountains are seen and described in general terms and in places as if from afar. Then the camera moves closer. The fourth chapter, entitled "A Near View of the High Sierra," recounts a narration of what purports to be a single experience of Muir's,[7] making concrete what has been generally described in the preceding three chapters. Actually, the fourth chapter is an amazing high point both for this book and for Muir's art as a whole. It is so nearly perfect as an allegory that it is hard not to see it as a conscious effort on Muir's part to define some of his ideas about the relative values of nature and art and to suggest, through poetic means, some of his own intensity of feeling about the High Sierra.

The chapter is organized around two anecdotes. In the first, Muir guides two artists to an "alpine landscape" suitable for sketching; in the second, he describes a three-day jaunt he took alone to the summit of Mount Ritter. The implied comparison could hardly be more pointed. The artists are described respectfully by Muir throughout, and yet they are obviously limited in their appreciation of the wild mountain scenery by the limitations of their craft. He leads them to the head of the upper Tuolumne River and is entranced by the reflection in their faces of the "fresh beauty" of the scenery. But they are disappointed by "the general expression of the scenery—rocky and savage," and they complain to him that "all this is huge and sublime, but we see nothing as yet at all available for effective pictures. Art is long, and art is limited, you know; and here are foregrounds, middle-grounds, backgrounds all alike" (I, 59-60). Muir, who tells them to "bide a wee," eventually produces a view which satisfies them. Then, with the artists settled down for a few days of sketching, he determines to push on for his first ascent of Mount Ritter. Having exhibited the picturesque, he is now ready to attempt the sublime.

The narration of his ascent of Mount Ritter, which includes one of the most horrendous passages in Muir's writing, provides a striking contrast to the low-pitched narration of his efforts to satisfy the artists. Having arrived 12,800 feet up at a nearly sheer wall, Muir gained a point halfway to the top and then found himself unable to move either up or down. The experience is described as triggering something approaching a mystic revelation. First he visualized the realistic consequences of his situation: "my doom appeared fixed. I *must* fall. There would be a moment of bewilderment, and then a lifeless rumble down the one general precipice to the glacier below."

Then came the reaction to that thought. He became "nerve-shaken for the first time since setting foot on the mountains," and his mind seemed to fill "with a stifling smoke." His bout with "the everlasting Nay" is brief, however, and it is quickly followed by the reassertion of the forces of life: "I seemed suddenly to become possessed of a new sense, The other self, bygone experience, instinct, or Guardian Angel,—call it what you will,—came forward and assumed control. Then my trembling muscles became firm again, every rift and flaw in the rock was seen as through a microscope, and my limbs moved with a positiveness and precision with which I seemed to have nothing at all to do. Had I been borne aloft upon wings, my deliverance could not have been more complete" (I, 75). The "strange influx of strength" easily carried him to the summit.

The panoramic landscape of the Sierra which follows upon this narrative completes the allegory of the chapter. Unlike the "framed" views desired by the two artists, the panorama unfolded by Muir from the peak of Mount Ritter is limitless, sublime. Still, he wrote, "the eye, rejoicing in its freedom, roves about the vast expanse, yet returns again and again to the *fountain* peaks [italics mine]." "Mountains are fountains," Muir wrote in *My First Summer in the Sierra*, "beginning places." He touches a paradox worthy of Oriental religion. Mountain peaks, which to the Western eye must seem culminations ("peaks" in the double sense), are to Muir "beginning places," because there, though the finite ends, the infinite begins. The view, bought mystically through his finite struggle with destruction, is the equivalent of the Zen achievement of total passivity, or the becoming, to use Emerson's phrase, of a "naked eyeball," unencumbered by flesh, rapt in spirituality. The experience which to Thoreau was occasioned by the return of spring to Walden Pond appears to Muir through the vertical thrust of his body to this "fountain peak." The means to the experience is far less important than the experience itself.

Muir's return to the camp of the artists gives him an opportunity to indulge in some half-hidden deprecations of their choice of "art" over the sublimity of wild nature. "They seemed unreasonably glad to see me," he noted, since he had been gone only three days. The passage of time would necessarily be the most striking point of opposition between those bound to the finite and the beholder of the infinite. But "now their curious troubles" were over. They packed their "precious sketches" and Muir led them back to the lowlands (I, 85). The irony of "unreasonably," "curious," and "precious" does not seem particularly well concealed, but apparently few people have noticed it. It bears out the assumption which I have made that the allegory of the chapter is intended to suggest exactly what it does—the relative incapacity of art to reach beyond its own limitations to the sublime opportunities given by wild nature.

After this episode of high excitement, the general description continues in the next four chapters. Muir described mountain passes, glacier lakes and meadows, and the mountain forests. Each chapter is given more to general than particular description, but becomes increasingly concrete. Then Muir passes to the great chapters of this book, as perfect in their attention to the infinity of the small as Chapter IV is of the great infinities of the mountains. These last chapters are each built on one or another of two themes: the ubiquity of certain small creatures who are at home in wild natural surroundings, or the experience by Muir in a fresh new way of a violent natural phenomenon. The first is the theme of the chapters on the Douglas squirrel, the water ouzel, the wild sheep, and the bee pastures of the Sierra; the second may be observed in Muir's descriptions of a wild storm, a flood, and Sierra thunderstorms. Each, in its own way, offers a variation on the theme of Chapter IV.

The motto of all of the chapters on the wild creatures of the Sierra might be taken from the chapter on wild sheep. All one need do to fit the following description of the difference between wild and tame sheep to the situation of the ouzel, the Douglas squirrel, or of any wild creature is to change a word or two.

The domestic sheep, Muir began, "is expressionless, like a dull bundle of something only half alive." The wild sheep, on the other hand, "is as elegant and graceful as a deer, every movement manifesting admirable strength and character." He then goes on to a general comparison of wildness and tameness, opposing what he believes to be the appropriate traits of each in several categories: "The tame is timid; the wild is bold. The tame is always more or less ruffled and dirty; while the wild is as smooth and clean as the flowers of the mountain pastures" (II, 38-39). The same comparison is implicit in the other chapters. The Douglas squirrel, the water ouzel, the bees and flowers of the bee pastures are all alive, "elegant and graceful," bold, and always, always clean. The Douglas squirrel, though he eats seeds from cones "dripping with soft balsam, and covered with prickles, and so strongly put together that a boy would be puzzled to cut them open with a jacknife," yet manages to dine on these cones "with easy dignity and cleanliness, making less effort apparently than a man would in eating soft cookery from a plate" (I, 267-68). The ouzel's nest is a triumph of bird architecture, revealing "no harsh lines [in] . . . any portion of the nest as seen in place" (II, 24). The flowers of the bee pastures in spring days seem to throb with life "beneath the life-giving sunshine," and plant growth is vibrant, "every bush and flower is seen as a hive of restless industry" (II, 106).

In each case the natural life of these creatures is opposed to something unnatural, and the results are as delightful as they are varied. For the Douglas squirrel, Muir describes an occasion when he accidentally engaged the attention of a Douglas by whistling. The squirrel stopped to listen to the new sound, and gradually gathered a crowd of wild creatures with him. Muir went through his repertoire: "Bonnie Doon," "Lass o' Gowrie," "O'er the Water to Charlie," and others, all of which seemed to command the respectful attention of his wild audience. Then he "ventured to give the 'Old Hundredth,'" and the entire audience, the Douglas leading the way, turned tail and ran, "leaving a somewhat profane impression, as if he had said, 'I'll be hanged if you get me to hear anything so solemn and unpiny'" (I, 269). When Muir repeated the experiment some years later, he obtained the same result.

He pictures the water ouzel flying within reach of flying chips produced by a woodchopper on the riverbank, the bird "cheerily singing" nevertheless. The ouzels remain as wild as the river to which they are somehow mystically attached. They sing on "through the din of the machinery, and all the noisy confusion of dogs, cattle, and workmen" in the sawmills of the lower reaches of "their" rivers (II, 27). Subtly, Muir leads the reader to the conclusion that the beauty and grace of these creatures is a function of their wildness, that this wildness is in constant opposition to the corruption of civilization, and that there is some element in all men which recognizes their beauty and naturalness. The culmination of his description of the water ouzel occurs through a lesser being, whom Muir magnificently characterizes as "a sort of foothill mountaineer." He is addicted to the killing of wild animals and birds to feed to his great lazy tomcat, but he cannot bring himself to shoot a water ouzel after he has once heard the bird sing (II, 30-31). The lesson is clear; however gross he may be, man may be spiritualized by contact with nature.

The three chapters on the terrible phenomena of nature—wind, storm, and flood—teach a different lesson. Muir, as I have said, was committed to the belief that "there is not . . . a mighty effort or the need of one, in wild Nature." He was dedicated to the contradiction of the belief not merely that cataclysmic events were evil but that they even occur. All nature is flow, he says again and again. What man fears as a violent interruption of his order (which he calls *disorder*) is actually still an orderly flow of a different but no less beautiful kind.

The best known of these chapters treats Muir's experience atop a Douglas spruce at the height of a wind storm, when the top of the tree is swaying in arcs of from twenty to thirty degrees. In the whole narrative there is no hint of violence. The images are all of sea waves; regularity; orderly and beautiful processions of colors, movements, and, above all, scents, carried by the wind. "The fragrance of the woods was less marked than that produced during a warm rain, when so many balsamic buds and leaves are steeped like tea; but, from the chafing of resiny branches against each other, and the incessant attrition of myriads of needles, the gale was spiced to a very tonic degree" (I, 283).

The wind becomes a perfect symbol under Muir's hand for unity in diversity. Constant, yet eternally changing in its degree, in the scents it carries, and in the memories it invokes, the wind may be for any man, in or out of wild nature, a means to lose self in the contemplation of the divine. To Muir the wind is never invisible: "Most people like to look at mountain rivers, and bear them in mind; but few care to look at the winds, though far more beautiful and sublime, and though they become at times about as visible as flowing water" (I, 285). He develops the parallel between mountain rivers and rivers of wind, and he concludes that the spectacle of "lace-like mountain streams" is "far less sublime and not a whit more substantial than what we may behold of these storm-streams of air in the mountain woods."

Movement is constant. T. S. Eliot may want to achieve "the still point of a turning world," but not John Muir. He is content with the revelation that the constancy of flow has no exceptions, that trees and men are more alike than the ordinary man believes. He therefore ends his description of the wind storm by pointing out this one lesson from his experience: "We all travel the milky way together, trees and men; but it never occurred to me until this storm-day, while swinging in the wind, that trees are travellers, in the ordinary sense. They make many journeys, not extensive ones, it is true; but our own journeys, away and back again, are only little more than tree-wavings— many of them not so much" (I, 286).

The descriptions of flood and thunderstorms are similarly reassuring. The thunderstorms are patterned and orderly, each producing the same effect: "everything is refreshed and invigorated, a stream of fragrance rises, and the storm is finished" (II, 4). The same is true of floods, but man in the lowlands is "confounded by a multitude of separate and apparently antagonistic impressions" of what is happening. If he will go to a high place, he will find that floods are perfectly orderly, controlled by "the topography of the regions where they rise and over which they pass" (I, 295-96). Muir goes to a ridge where he can watch the effects of the flood and, as he ascends, notes that the "partial, confusing effects disappear and the phenomena are beheld united and harmonious." Upon returning to the lowland, the paradox is completed. The "good people" of the village pity his "bedraggled condition as if I were some benumbed castaway snatched from the sea, while I, in turn, warm with the excitement and reeking like the ground, pitied them for being dry and defrauded of all the glory that Nature had spread round about them that day" (I, 301).

The total effect of *The Mountains of California* is certainly greater than the sum of its parts. Sections of general description are accurate and sensitive, and the descriptions of animals and natural phenomena might be compared without discredit to similar lowland experiences in *Walden*. Added to these, the intensity of Muir's personal ecstasies, both in the heights and through his sympathies with the natural inhabitants of the Sierra, heightens both the external narrative interest of the volume and its philosophical impact. But the total effect is more than these. It is comparable (and here I must seem dreadfully romantic and uncritical) to the effect of reading a particularly personal lyric poem, if one can forget the immense differences of length and matter. For all the careful marshaling of fact in the narration, from exact and estimated measurements of heights and distance to carefully documented citations from learned authors on ranges of animals, species and genera of plants discussed, this is above all a *personal* book. It is also an artful book. Under the cloak of verisimilitude that accompanies any story of personal narration, Muir has ordered and invented incidents and anecdotes to produce an effect as artistically contrived as any lyric.

There is nothing dishonest in such an ordering and, where necessary, invention. We must grant that Muir's own feelings about wild nature are honestly derived and honestly held. His whole life is a document to that effect. As an artist, as, primarily, a poet, he has the right, indeed, the obligation to make clear not the externals of his experience so much as those most deeply held emotions which can only be felt, not understood. The effect of Chapter Four, of the chapters on storms, and of the consideration of the Douglas squirrel, the ouzel, the wild sheep is a poetic effect. A certain amount of information is gained, to be sure, but one takes away primarily a sensation of the whole-ness of nature from these descriptions and a belief that it is only in wild nature that one can exercise the power of what Emerson called the "reason" to comprehend the unity of creation.

One example of how Muir has changed his experience for pre-sentation in this volume illustrates his artistic technique. A section from Chapter III, describing the "snow-banners" of the Sierra peaks, is drawn from an experience described fully in his journal. The journal account begins with an emphasis on wind and its effect on trees, proceeds to a specific narration of where and how Muir went to observe the snow-banners, and then describes the phenomenon in a mixture of specific detail of each banner and generalizations about their appearance. The description of two of the banners is a curious blend of scientific observation and esthetic judgment: "The banner from Mount Clark was broad and variable, the breadth increasing with the distance from the point of attachment. That from Gray Mountain was the finest, the attachment delicate and clear, and the widening of the swaying sheet regular" (*John of the Mountains,* 139-40).

In the text in *The Mountains of California,* the description, much enlarged, begins instead with a consideration of the life-cycle of snow. Mountain snow, Muir wrote, has a more interesting life than snow "which falls into the tranquil depths of the forest." When it falls on exposed slopes it may be whirled upward again and again in the snow-banners until it is "locked fast in bossy drifts, or in the wombs of glaciers, some of it to remain silent and rigid for centuries before it is finally melted and sent singing down the mountain-sides to the sea." The central stress of the image is on the orderly or cyclical processes of nature.

These orderly processes are then compared with the rare occasions when nature uses these same materials for a display, not of disorder, though the operating agent is a storm, but of a transcendent peak of beauty. Muir wrote that he had been waiting for an opportunity to examine closely another phenomenon, the production of an ice-cone at the base of Upper Yosemite Fall; and he was setting out on that purpose when he observed the snow-banners above him. "So rare and splendid a phenomenon, of course, overbore all other considerations," he adds, suggesting that the banners are only the most exciting of a plenitude of wonders. He then moves to a sufficient height and surveys the scene. His technique is at once both more specific and more general than the technique used in the journal. He makes no comparison between the beauties of individual peaks, no effort to gauge the relation between length and breadth of individual banners. He does bring the reader into the description: "Fancy yourself standing on this Yosemite ridge looking eastward." He also paints in the foreground and middle-ground leading to the center of interest, the banners themselves, with an eye toward increasing the contrast. Then, though the mountain peaks are not specified as they were in the journal account, he gives a detailed description of the appearance of one generalized banner. He concludes by shutting out the foreground: "These are the main features of the beautiful and terrible picture as seen from the forest window; and it would still be surpassingly glorious were the fore- and middle-grounds obliterated alto-gether, leaving only the black peaks, the white banners, and the blue sky" (I, 47-53).

With hardly a false note, Muir transformed an isolated exper-ience into one belonging to the processes of the mountains, standing as a kind of esthetic summit to the cycle of fall, evaporation, and fall of the snow. He has also succeeded in com-municating a vision only sketched out in his journal in such a way that the description in *The Mountains of California* is meaningful even to someone who has never been to the mountains. A small example, perhaps, but it is typical of the total effect produced by his manipulation of materials in the book as a whole.

Many other examples could be summoned to suggest how art-fully the book was written. To see *The Mountains of California* as a Baedeker for geologists and naturalists and just plain tourists is to see it incorrectly. It is more a Transcendental lyric poem, with wild nature and the wild creatures and phenomena of the Sierra as its subjects. Muir, as a character in the book, is a narrator coming of age in terms of his esthetic experiences of wildness. Muir, as the author, is a controlling and artistically unifying force, changing, inventing, and rearranging his own experiences to fit the artistic demands of the book.

VI   *Nature Is a Crab*

William F. Badé collected a group of Muir's ephemeral writ-ings of about the same period as the periodical pieces which went into *The Mountains of California* and published them in Volume VIII of the Sierra Edition of Muir's works under the general title of *Steep Trails* (1918). This volume supplements *The Mountains of California* by ranging farther afield to Utah, Nevada, Oregon, and Washington and also by stressing complementary aspects of wilderness life. Of the twenty-four essays included in the volume, twenty are almost purely de-scriptive, but even these have their moments of reflection and Transcendental perception. The other four essays on Mount Shasta and its environs, and especially the first article, entitled "Wild Wool," are among the most interesting and revealing of Muir's works.

Badé chose to violate his own decision to arrange the chapters of *Steep Trails* chronologically by placing "Wild Wool" first in the volume.[8] And well he might. Though most of the rest of the book has a limited interest, "Wild Wool" deserves comparison with the best essays of Thoreau. The subject of the essay seems to be a comparison of the fineness of the wool of a wild sheep with the wool of domesticated sheep, but this "subject" soon becomes a useful symbol in a more general discussion of the opposition of nature and culture. Structurally, rhetorically, philosophically, it is the finest short article Muir ever wrote.

Muir seems to open the essay obliquely with a paragraph about a "friend" who is a true believer in "culture," who "cultivates" every "bog, rock, and moorland" he can plough. But the obliqueness is only apparent, for Muir is setting up an opposition between wildness and cultivation which later becomes central to the essay. The paragraph is full of puns and paradoxes through which the degree of Muir's opposition to his friend's feelings is made clear.

> Moral improvers have calls to preach. I have a friend who has a call to plough, and woe to the daisy sod or azalea thicket that falls under the savage redemption of his keen steel shares. Not content with the so-called subjugation of every terrestrial bog, rock, and moorland, he would fain discover some method of reclamation applicable to the ocean and the sky, that in due calendar time they might be brought to bud and blossom as the rose. Our efforts are of no avail when we seek to turn his attention to wild roses, or to the fact that both ocean and sky are already about as rosy as possible—the one with stars, the other with dulse, and foam, and wild light. The practical developments of his culture are orchards and clover-fields wearing a smiling, benevolent aspect, truly excellent in their way, though a near view discloses something barbarous in them all. Wildness charms not my friend, charm it never so wisely: and whatsoever may be the character of his heaven, his earth seems only a chaos of agricultural possibilities calling for grubbing hoes and manures.
>
> (3-4)

Whoever posed for this portrait specifically, if anyone did, the general outline obviously comes from Muir's father, whose feelings about the relative merits of wild nature and culture closely correspond to this rather idealized view. The metaphor of "redemption" of nature through the offices of the plough is also appropriate to Muir's father particularly.

With the character of the comparison thus firmly established, Muir then produces a symbol for the side of culture which reminds the reader of Frost's opposition in "Mending Wall."

When Muir attempts to defend wildness to his friend, "he good-naturedly shakes a big mellow apple in my face, reiterating his favorite aphorism, 'Culture is an orchard apple; Nature is a crab.' " To Muir, such a heinous philosophy demands refutation, but his friend seems to be on sure ground for his opinion, at least when within the confines of his own orchard. Muir then shifts the subject (again, only apparently) to a discovery he made while accompanying some friends who were hunting wild sheep near Mount Shasta. He finds, to controvert his culture-conscious friend, that the wool of the wild sheep of the Mount Shasta region is much finer than that of cultivated ones. "Here," says Muir, "is an argument for fine wildness that needs no explanation. Not that such arguments are by any means rare, for all wildness is finer than tameness, but because fine wool is appreciable by everybody alike—from the most speculative president of national wool-growers' associations all the way down to the gude-wife spinning by her ingleside" (4-5).

After a thorough analysis of the fineness of the wool of wild sheep, in which he puns often on the words "fine" and "tame," Muir is ready to return to the central argument: the opposition of nature and culture. He complains first that "it seems well-nigh impossible to obtain a hearing on behalf of nature from any other standpoint than that of human use." Thus the argument that the wool from domesticated sheep would not keep a wild sheep alive for a winter is falsely denied by the advocates of culture (11). Muir complains that their chop-logic is a product of the assumption that "the world is made especially for the uses of man," even though "every animal, plant, and crystal controverts it in the plainest terms" (12).

To this point the essay has proceeded in a manner very similar to discussions of the same topic in *A Thousand-Mile Walk*. Then, almost casually, Muir takes the one further step necessary to redeem the wilderness side of the argument, changing what had been to this point a bantering of opposite points of view into a flash of revelation of Transcendental profundity. He begins in opposition to the doctrine of use. Use implies subordination, but Muir instead finds in nature a coordinating principle:

> I have never yet happened upon a trace of evidence that seemed to show that any one animal was ever made for another as much as it was made for itself. Not that Nature manifests any such thing as selfish isolation. In the making of every animal the presence of every other animal has been recognized. Indeed,

every atom in creation may be said to be acquainted with and married to every other, but with universal union there is a division sufficient in degree for the purposes of the most intense individuality; no matter, therefore, what may be the note which any creature forms in the song of existence, it is made first for itself, then more and more remotely for all the world and worlds.   (12)

This coordination of diversity adequately explains two paradoxes which Muir marshalls in support of an argument to follow: if nature did not individualize the atoms of the universe, it "would be felted together like a fleece of tame wool." But, "we are governed more than we know, and most when we are wildest" (12-13). How? Muir invokes Darwin, as he did in *A Thousand-Mile Walk*, but it is a Transcendental Darwin, whose nature "red in tooth and claw" is organized and coordinated: "Plants, animals, and stars are all kept in place, bridled along appointed ways, *with* one another, and *through the midst* of one another—killing and being killed, eating and being eaten, in harmonious proportions and quantities [italics Muir's]." So far so good, but what is man's place in this schema? Muir answers, with a magnificent insight, that he is perfectly in place, that "it is right that we should thus reciprocally make use of one another, rob, cook, and consume, to the utmost of our healthy appetites and desires" (13).

"Cultivation" and its derivative, "culture," are to man exactly as refinement of appetite is to a wild animal. "When a hawk pounces upon a linnet and proceeds to pull out its feathers, preparatory to making a meal, the hawk may be said to be cultivating the linnet, and he certainly does effect an improvement as far as hawkfood is concerned; but what of the songster?" (13-14). What poses as "culture" is merely the first step in the process of eating, not at all different from the situation of the hawk and the linnet, or, to recur to Muir's earlier example from *A Thousand-Mile Walk*, of the alligator and the man. "We eat wild oysters alive with great directness, waiting for no cultivation, and leaving scarce a second of distance between the shell and the lip; but we take wild sheep home and subject them to the many extended processes of husbandry, and finish by boiling them in a pot" (14). The two processes, Muir concludes, are identical. The sheep is dead to nature the minute the domestication process begins with him. Eating him only completes the job. Muir then brings the apple and the sheep together to conclude the argument. The wild apple tree is a fine thing in nature, most men will admit, in every aspect except the quantity of its fruit.

> Man, therefore, takes the tree from the woods, manures and prunes and grafts, plans and guesses, adds a little of this and that, selects and rejects, until apples of every conceivable size and softness are produced, like nut-galls in response to the irritating punctures of insects. Orchard apples are to me the most eloquent words that culture has ever spoken, but they reflect no imperfection upon Nature's spicy crab. Every cultivated apple is a crab, not improved, *but cooked* [italics Muir's], variously softened and swelled out in the process, mellowed, sweetened, spiced, and rendered pulpy and foodful, but as utterly unfit for the uses of nature as a meadowlark killed and plucked and roasted. Give to nature every cultured apple—codling, pippin, russet—and every sheep so laboriously compounded—muffled Southdowns, hairy Cotswolds, wrinkled Merinos—and she would throw the one to her caterpillars, the other to her wolves.   (15-16)

The argument is unanswerable in the terms in which it is given. Conditions as unlike as wild and tame sheep, wild and cultured apples, may not be compared, since tameness is a state of controlled death, in terms of adaptability to nature. Surely, after reading this essay, one need never ask why Muir preferred to live in the wild.

In "Wild Wool," Muir brings his most striking powers of rhetoric—irony, control of paradox, brilliant insight into semantic obfuscation of the question—to the destruction of a concept which he hated with his whole soul. His parallels, analogies, and metaphors are precisely chosen for their purpose in the argument. Although Muir's style at times resembles Thoreau's, the essay as a whole is perfectly original. The perfection of this one essay more than redeems the rather pedestrian writing in many of the other essays included in *Steep Trails*.

VII *The National Parks Again*

The association of Muir with the editors of *Scribner's Monthly*, Richard Watson Gilder and Robert Underwood Johnson, was doubly responsible for the publication of *The Mountains of California*. First, much of the material included within the book was originally published in that periodical. But even more important, the influence of Muir upon Johnson in particular moved the wheels of government to the creation of Yosemite National

Park, thereby freeing Muir from one of his primary commitments and allowing him to devote time to his book.

I have showed that Muir's non-glacial early writings were all directed to the cause of conservation of the mountain wilderness of California. In the editors of *Scribner's Monthly* he found allies to his cause far beyond his highest expectations. Both outspoken and influential (Gilder was a close personal friend of Grover Cleveland, and, through him, of later Presidents as well), the editors of *Scribner's Monthly* liked nothing better than a good cause to which they could add the weight of their magazine, thereby spurring civic virtue and circulation at the same time. But they were probably not aware while they were publishing Muir's early articles on the Sierra that they were furthering the cause of conservation. That awareness did not come until nearly ten years after the articles were published when Robert Underwood Johnson made a trip to California and, so he believed, "proposed to Muir that we should set on foot the project of the Yosemite National Park."

Muir's capacity as a diplomat may amusingly be construed from Johnson's account of that memorable meeting. The subject of the denudation of the mountain pastures by sheep was casually broached by Muir, whereupon Johnson said, "obviously the thing to do is to make a Yosemite National Park around the valley on the plan of the Yellowstone."[9] Muir was "skeptical," but Johnson "persisted" to the point of "convincing" Muir to write two articles for *The Century* (the magazine's name since 1881) to set the project in motion. On October 1, 1890, one month after the appearance of Muir's second article, Yosemite National Park became a fact.[10] Such was the influence of *The Century Magazine* and its brilliant associate editor, however naïve Johnson appeared in the hands of crafty old John Muir.

The founding of Yosemite National Park did not end Muir's efforts toward national control over the Sierra. There was still the problem of California's control since 1866 of the valley of the Yosemite itself. Set right in the middle of the National Park, and one-thirty-fifth its size, the California-controlled section of the park soon became an eyesore—though it was blessed with perhaps the greatest natural beauty of the region—in comparison to the better-managed national park. Muir hardly rested from his so-easily crowned labors to create Yosemite National Park before he set out to have California recede the control of the Valley of the Yosemite to the National Park Service.

Our National Parks (1901) was compiled by Muir primarily to aid in that cause. A review of the areas which had been set aside as national parks, with emphasis on Yosemite, the book is somewhat less interesting than *The Mountains of California;* but parts of it are as good as anything Muir ever wrote. The book opens, for example, with a fine paragraph about how "thousands of tired, nerve-shaken, over-civilized people are beginning to find out that going to the mountains is going home." Muir is not of one mind about the value of nature "mixed with spectacles, silliness, and kodaks" to tourists "arrayed more gorgeously than scarlet tanagers, frightening the wild game with red umbrellas" (3-4). He has no doubt however, that experience of wild nature, however regimented and ill-considered, will eventually prove meaningful to even the most casual tourist.

The first three chapters are considerations of Western national parks in general, Yellowstone, and Yosemite. These chapters, though reflective in part, are mostly limited to the functions of the guidebook. Succeeding chapters on the forests, wild gardens, animals, birds, and the fountains and streams of the Yosemite give Muir a better opportunity to display his sympathy and immense knowledge of these particulars of the area he loved so well. The chapter on Sequoia and General Grant National parks provides him with an opportunity for a hymn to the beauty of "Nature's forest masterpiece and . . . the greatest of all living things," the sequoia (290).

The last chapter, "The American Forests," shows Muir at his polemical best. He begins with a titanic catalog of the range and growth of the American forests, from East Coast to West, "planted in groves, and belts, and broad exuberant mantling forests, with the largest, most varied, most fruitful, and most beautiful trees in the world" (357). There is such a plenitude in the American forests that "nobody need have cared had there been no pines in Norway, no cedars and deodars in Lebanon and the Himalayas, no vine-clad selvas in the basin of the Amazon." But, though "a great delight to God," the forests of America have been "slighted by man." The picture Muir has presented was only true centuries ago when only the Indian's stone axe, the beaver's teeth, and fires caused by lightning provided threats to the American forest. So-called "civilization" now threatens to destroy the forests entirely. Muir points out that "every other civilized nation in the world has been compelled to care for its forests." Prussia, France, Switzerland, Russia, Japan, and India are all far ahead of the United States in this respect.

Muir describes the weak and unenforceable laws protecting the forests, lists some of the destructive forces which had wreaked havoc upon them (including the "hoofed locusts" with which he was so familiar), but always ends with the great villain in his view of cosmic order—unfeeling, thoughtless man. One of the few extensive dialogues in his writing is brought in to support his argument, a conversation among some "drifting adventurers" of California who made their living by a systematic rape of the beauties of nature. This conversation is reported factually, supplying its own ironic overtones through its context, as may be seen in this example:

> "Boys, as soon as this job's done I'm goin' into the duck business. There's big money in it, and your grub costs nothing. Tule Joe made five hundred dollars last winter on mallard and teal. Shot 'em on the Joaquin, tied 'em in dozens by the neck, and shipped 'em to san Francisco. And when he was tired of wading in the sloughs and touched with rheumatiz, he just knocked off on ducks and went to the Contra Costa hills for dove and quail. It's a mighty good business, and you're your own boss, and the whole thing's fun." (380-81)

"Happy robbers!" Muir comments, "dwelling in the most beautiful woods, in the most salubrious climate, breathing delightful odors both day and night," and pillaging the land that gives them these pleasures (383). "Any fool can destroy trees," Muir concluded his argument. Though "God has cared for these trees, saved them from drought, disease, avalanches, and a thousand straining, leveling tempests and floods . . . he cannot save them from fools,—only Uncle Sam can do that" (392-93). As ever, Muir is urging the change of law from an unnatural to a natural one. The destruction of forests by natural causes is something which he and nature can always take in stride. But man suffers from an unnatural, shortsighted foolishness and therefore required the inhibition of law to abate his stupidity.

VIII *A Baedeker to Boil the Pot*

In 1911 Robert Underwood Johnson requested Muir, on behalf of the Century Publishing Company, of which *The Century Magazine* was a part, to gather together some of his writings about the Yosemite for a book. Muir probably looked upon the request as an obligation to an old friend—a friend who had been instrumental in saving the Yosemite by having it declared a national park. Muir's first book, *The Mountains of California,* had been published originally by Century Company, but Muir had shifted his allegiance to Houghton Mifflin Company for *My First Summer in the Sierra,* as he had contributed articles to the Boston periodical, *The Atlantic Monthly.* Now Johnson seemed to be requesting this new book somewhat for old times' sake—and also because a guide book to Yosemite written by John Muir might expect a considerable sale!

Muir acceded to Johnson's request, but he was unwilling to put much effort into the book. About one-third of the book is a reprinting from *The Mountains of California.* What is new is not among Muir's best writing, by and large.[11] Chapter I, "The Approach to the Valley," is a workmanlike introduction to its salient features. Chapter II is a brief but striking glimpse of the Yosemite in a storm, as usual provoking some fine description from Muir. Chapters V, X, and XI summarize commentaries found in more artistic form elsewhere about the trees of the valley, South Dome, and the glacial origin of Yosemite. Chapter XII is actually a guide to one-, two-, and three-day excursions in Yosemite, with suggestions for longer hikes. Chapters XIII and XIV memorialize two of the pioneers of Yosemite, Lamon and Galen Clark. The last chapter, Chapter XV, is specifically intended to urge the preservation of Hetch Hetchy Valley from exploitation, a lost cause which darkened Muir's last years.

The Yosemite, with the exception of a few striking anecdotes, is probably the least artistic and, as a whole, the least interesting of Muir's books. Published just the year before *The Story of My Boyhood and Youth,* it proves that even Muir could be bored with descriptions of scenes which had delighted him for more than forty years. Fortunately, he had his youth and his travels in Alaska to work on during his last years.

IX *Earning a Living*

In the interest of taking up Muir's writings as they first appear in his journals and following them through to their conclusion in print and in their didactic effect upon the National Parks movement, I have taken considerable liberties with the chronology of Muir's life. During the 1870's, Muir extended his Western explorations through Utah, Nevada, Oregon, and Washington. He also made increasingly frequent visits to the Strentzel household in the Alhambra Valley, visits which were capped on April 14, 1880, with his marriage to Louie Wanda Strentzel.

At first glance, Muir does not seem to have been a marriage-able man, but such was not the case. A welter of contradictions, he was, in spite of his love of freedom, naturally gregarious. The "cold shadows of loneliness" which accompanied him when he first set out on his one-thousand mile walk were quite as im-portant to him as a motive to return to the lowlands as was his dependence upon bread. He became, in spite of his com-pelling wanderlust, something of a model husband. Certainly the success which he had during the decade of the 1880's as a provider for his family testifies to his capacity as husband and husbandman. His fruit ranch cleared $10,000 a year for ten years. When he went on the Harriman Alaska expedition in 1899, Muir believed that this experience had made him richer than Harriman himself: "I have all the money I want and he hasn't."[12]

One of the by-products of Muir's marriage was his connection with the publication of *Picturesque California,* an elaborately illustrated and pretentiously published guide to the natural beauties of California and of the Pacific Coast as far north as Alaska. Sold by subscription in parts, it is representative of a lucrative form of publishing that is no longer, fortunately, as popular as it was at the end of the nineteenth century. Muir accepted the editorship of the series in 1887, doubtless as a means of keeping his hand in writing and for the occasional opportunities it afforded to venture into the wilds of California in search of the picturesque. Six of his own essays appear in the two large folio volumes, but none of them is distinctive except for one essay on Mount Shasta. His editorial work for the volume must have been a drain on a man who hated the thought of "narrowing my attention to bookmaking out of material I have already eaten and drunken."

The editorship of *Picturesque California* does stand as testi-mony to Muir's fame six years before his first book, *Mountains of California,* was published. In the interest of taking up Muir's writings in their most permanent form, I have followed a combined chronology of book publication dates plus the order of Muir's experiences. By 1887, though he had written no books, Muir had been a constant contributor to magazines and newspapers, and his reputation was based entirely on these ephemera. He was already "John o' Mountains" to a large public who had read his letters to various California papers, listened to his lectures, or read his longer, more reflective essays in various magazines. To 1879, these essays were primarily concerned with wildness in California; but his love of the wilderness led him in 1879, and frequently thereafter, to explorations of the vaster wilderness of Alaska.

CHAPTER 5

In the Glacial Laboratory

MUIR'S ACCOUNTS of his five journeys to Alaska form a curiously uneven and often disappointing epilogue to the volumes concerning his rambles in California. One might expect that the sublimities of that subcontinent, built on a backbone of mountains higher than those of California and carved eternally anew by glaciers infinitely grander than any Muir had ever seen, would bring out only the best of his writing. But, though Alaska's natural wonders profoundly affected him, his descriptions rarely rise to the heights of fine prose found nearly everywhere in his California books.

In fact, many of the same elements which made Muir's Alaskan experiences so moving to him made his descriptions of his experiences less effective. It is possible to maintain a feeling of sublimity for a long time in the presence of repeated heightened emotion; it is almost impossible to describe the same circumstances and feelings. Peaks of experience in *The Mountains of California* are made more effective by comparison with foothills and prairies of description less intense. In Muir's Alaskan travels, he for many days at a time moved from crest to crest, discovering each day new and, so he tries to tell us, more sublime visions of rock and ice. Even the most sympathetic reader—even the one who has experienced the grandeur of Alaskan scenery and knows exactly what Muir is attempting to express—cannot but feel his failure. Though we may once have attained a similar constant rapture, when reading of it in another, we must admit our earthbound condition.

A second reason for the comparative failure of Muir's Alaskan books is a function of the terrible harshness of the Alaskan climate. Muir began *My First Summer in the Sierra* with a sentence that was made particularly meaningful to him by his Alaskan experiences: "In the great Central Valley of California there are only two seasons—spring and summer." In *Travels in Alaska* he remarked several times that there are only two seasons there, too: a ten-month winter and a two-month summer, with a very negligible spring and fall. The difference in climate produced a difference in tone between his Alaska and his California books. The California descriptions have a timeless quality, unrestricted and transcendental. All of his Alaskan travels are hurried by the seasons. A glacier is "lost" because the party must return to Fort Wrangell before the storms break; Muir's second visit must be cut short to allow him to catch a late-season steamer back to California; Muir's status as a lover of storms is forced to bow to the greater power of the climate of the North Polar Regions.

Third, the size and the comparative inaccessibility of Alaska worked against the success of his writing. Muir came to know intimately the details of the California wilderness. In Alaska he was always a tourist—a remarkably intelligent and perceptive tourist, but a tourist nonetheless. On all of his trips he was dependent upon water transportation to some degree. How shackling that dependence was he revealed in a letter to Samuel Hall Young concerning his trip on the *Corwin* in 1881. "There have been no mountains to climb," he wrote, "although I have had entrancing long-distance views of many. I have not had a chance to visit any glaciers. . . . Of God's process of modeling the world I saw but little—nothing for days but that limitless, relentless ice-pack. I was confined within the narrow prison of the ship; I had no freedom, I went at the will of other men; not of my own."[1] His situation aboard the *Corwin* was an extreme case, but it was to some degree typical of all his Alaskan trips.

With these reservations, one ought fairly to state that the two longer volumes of descriptions of Alaska nevertheless achieve a very high quality as literature. It is only in comparison with Muir's other writings that they may be said to fail.[2] They are certainly not merely "travel books," pure and simple. A reader coming to them before reading the California books would find them as comparable to the works of Thoreau in their sympathy with nature as any of Muir's writing. If they are of a lower order than some of his other books, it is because those books are of a very high order indeed.

I *Two Ministers*

In May, 1879, "anxious to gain some knowledge of the regions to the northward" of the Sierra Nevada of California which he had been studying for eleven years, Muir took passage aboard the steamer *Dakota*, "without any definite plans, as with the exception of a few of the Oregon peaks and their forests all the wild north was new" to him (*Travels in Alaska*, 3). In July he arrived, via the monthly mail boat, at Fort Wrangell, where he met for the first time the man with whom he was to share many of his Alaskan adventures, Samuel Hall Young.

The unusual nature of Muir's experiences in Alaska may perhaps best be seen in this single aspect of them—that they were all shared, that they were shared by one man, and that the sharer has left an account of them. Even more unusual is the fact that the sharer came to know the wilderness described by Muir, in some respects, better than he. Furthermore, the account Young left of their shared experiences, most judges would agree, is certainly more readable and perhaps even better literature than Muir's. The best technique of analysis of the first two parts of *Travels in Alaska*, therefore, seems to be a comparison with Young's *Alaska Days with John Muir*.

The three problems Muir faced in the writing of *Travels in Alaska* which I have discussed were not problems to Young. His experiences with Muir were his introduction to the sublime, and he managed to retain the freshness of the description of the new in his account. The restrictions of climate were no problem because he had no California to compare them with. And all his experiences seemed perfectly free and untrammeled —again because he had not Muir's more perfect freedom for comparison. He also had the immense advantage of a coherent subject—John Muir—for his book, which Muir had only indirectly. Still, his account is measurably better than Muir's on three points that are not dependent upon these advantages: structure, emphasis, and selection of incident.

Muir's account has only his own tried and true chronological organization to support it. Though there is some thematic development, which I shall discuss later, it is not fully developed and must be read between the lines. By and large, Muir recounts in a straightforward chronology the events of 1879 and 1880. Young's account is more subtle and artistic. Though he follows the chronology generally, he weaves in and out of it the two main themes of the adventures as he saw them. What he wrote of their first trip together is true of his whole book: "The voyage naturally divides itself into the human interest and the study of nature; yet the two constantly blended throughout the whole voyage" (71). Muir chose to "blend" human interest and nature study in his account; Young separated them so well that the points he wanted to make about each are emphasized.

Not that Young's emphasis is always in the best taste. His desire to pack his volume with "human interest" led him to the inclusion of several anecdotes that Muir wisely excluded. A case in point is a useless anecdote which Young seems to have printed only because he was a Wooster College graduate and had the normal Eastern collegian's inferior feelings about Harvard. He writes of how, "before starting on the voyage, we heard that there was a Harvard graduate . . . living among the Kake Indians on Kouyou Island." Imagine his surprise when arriving at the island he discovers eight Indian men "all dressed in colored four-dollar blankets," with the exception of the Harvard man, who had only a "filthy, two-dollar Hudson Bay blanket" (75-76). Or again, his description of an idiot son of an Indian chief is dragged out for its sentimental value far beyond the bounds of good taste and the purposes of his book (79-81).

More often, his selection of incidents for emphasis is more acute than Muir's. Both writers narrate in detail the fear suffered by their Indian paddlers during the approach to Glacier Bay. Muir summarizes the motives for their fear too brusquely: "After supper, crouching about a dull fire of fossil wood, they became still more doleful, and talked in tones that accorded well with the wind and waters and growling torrents about us, telling sad old stories of crushed canoes, drowned Indians, and hunters frozen in snowstorms" (178). Young spins out the narration at greater length, adding the touch of the supernatural which is needed to account for the violence of the Indians' fears on the next day. One arm of the bay has a fierce devil-fish "with arms as long as a tree, lurking in malignant patience, awaiting the passage that way of an unwary canoe." Another bay is guarded by the *Koosta-kah*, a mischievous fairy, half-otter, half-man, who delights in transporting sleeping humans miles away. A third arm of the bay harbors a killer whale which gulps whole canoes in one mouthful (100-1). Muir probably was loath to repeat such stories, but Young felt, properly, that they were needed to provide motivation for the actions of the Indians on the following day.

Other omissions by Muir are hard to explain. Two of the most lively passages of his Alaskan journals were omitted in *Travels in Alaska,* one on Indian superstition and another on the Indians' use of blankets as a medium of exchange and as symbols of prestige. Who would not wish that he had included some form of the following passage?

> A man's wealth is measured in blankets. "He is rich, he has five hundred blankets." The raising of a carved heraldic monument is a grand occasion. Some of the monuments cost as high as three hundred blankets, plus the cost of a grand entertainment and pot latch, when all are fed and receive presents. Occasionally a rich Indian holds a grand potlatch, giving away all the hard-earned savings of a lifetime. Then he becomes a chief, or Tyee. A good way to get rid of riches in old age when from their kind they are hard to keep. It is the common price of fame and power.   (*John of the Mountains,* 273)

Occasionally Muir's narrative suffers from the inclusion of too many incidents. Anyone who has ever heard the sounds made by a seacoast glacier when icebergs are being "calved" from it knows that it is one of the most awesome events in nature. Thunder Bay is well named for the phenomenon. Muir's description is detailed, scientific, and, in his efforts to include the variety of the phenomena, relatively dull. His emphasis, as ever, is on the continuousness of the process, but in placing it there he loses the magnificence of the event. It is all too orderly, too objective, too much seen as process and not occurrence:

> When a large mass sinks from the upper fissured portion of the wall, there is first a keen, prolonged, thundering roar, which slowly subsides into a low, muttering growl, followed by numerous smaller gratings, clashing sounds from the agitated bergs that dance in the waves about the newcomer as if in welcome; and these again are followed by the swash and roar of the waves that are raised and hurled up to beach against the moraines. But the largest and most beautiful of the bergs, instead of thus falling from the upper weathered portion of the wall, rise from the submerged portion with a still grander commotion, springing with tremendous voice and gestures nearly to the top of the wall, tons of water streaming like hair down their sides, plunging and rising again and again before they finally settle in perfect poise, free at last, after having formed part of the slow-

crawling glacier for centuries. And as we contemplate their history, as they sail calmly away down the fiord to the sea, how wonderful it seems that ice formed from pressed snow on the far-off mountains two or three hundred years ago should still be pure and lovely in color after all its travel and toil in the rough mountain quarries, grinding and fashioning the features of predestined landscapes. (324-25)

Young presents only one example of iceberg production (Muir has several others besides the one quoted), and in his single example one has to read deeply to see that the process is going on eternally. His "one iceberg" moves dramatically toward freedom from its parent glacier. He writes of how he observed its line of fracture suddenly appearing in "two deep lines of prussian blue"; how "this great pyramid of blue-veined onyx" leaned further and further toward the sea, "until it became a tower of Pisa"; how, "breathless and anxious," he waited for it to split off until "its long delay became almost a greater strain than I could bear. I jumped up and down and waved my arms and shouted at the glacier to 'hurry up.'" Finally, "the great tower of crystal shot up into the air two hundred feet or more." For Young had decided to describe one of the "largest and most beautiful of the bergs," as Muir put it, which makes its commotion by buoyancy instead of by gravity. But for Young this entirely natural process, the springing up of the berg, is a "surprising climax," and his description gives it all of the advantages of novelty as well as majesty.

Events then follow fast in his description, but there is only one hint that the process which he is describing is continual: "Its great weight of thousands of tons, falling from such a height, splashed great sheets of water high into the air, and a rainbow of wondrous brilliance flashed and vanished. A mighty wave swept majestically down the bay, rocking the massive bergs like corks, and, breaking against my granite pillar, tossed its spray half-way up to my lofty perch" (151-53). Only the reference to the "massive bergs" in the bay suggests that the incident described was not unique. Young's account is, in a sense, less honest than Muir's because it exaggerates the individuality of the experience. Yet no one would say that it is the less effective of the two as pure description.

The most telling difference between the two accounts is in the incidents in which Muir figures as a hero. As I stated earlier, in the chapter on *A Thousand Mile Walk*, Muir suffers as a writer for his successes as a man. Nowhere is this better seen than in the two accounts of his saving Young's life. Muir would not have included the anecdote in his text at all had not an amazingly corrupt account of it appeared already in a popular magazine.[3] As it is, he hurries through the narrative, modestly skipping aspects of it which Young put to good use in his own account. The details of Muir's strength and bravery which Young gives—his carrying his companion, disabled with two dislocated arms, down several thousand feet of sheer mountain walls—make Young's narrative believable and poignant. Their absence in Muir's account is simply provoking. Muir probably should not have included the anecdote at all. A story like that simply cannot be told well by the hero of it. Alas, that was a condition which, in the nature of things, Muir could not escape.

II *Doctrine and Transcendence*

Muir and Young became the closest of friends during their months together. Young's love of Muir reached the level of adoration. He called Muir his "Master" in understanding of the workings of God in nature (13). He sympathetically regarded Muir's "theism" as a devout and honest belief (97), and he commented finally that "to no other man do I feel that I owe so much; for I was blind and he made me see" (222). On Muir's side, he everywhere expressed his respect for Young as a person; but, hidden in his account of their months together, there is a peculiar dichotomy in his feelings toward the man Young and the doctrine Young espoused.

Consider the situation. After a few brief expeditions in the immediate neighborhood of Fort Wrangell, the two men set off together on a voyage in which science and theology, doctrine and its transcendence, were to work hand in hand. Young was to "locate and visit the tribes and villages of Thlingets to the north and west of Wrangell," and, "with the eager zeal of an Eliot or a Martin," to tell them "for the first time the Good News" of the gospel. Muir's mission was to find and study the forests, mountains, and glaciers of the coast. Young added, "I also was eager to see these and learn about them, and Muir was glad to study the natives with me—so our plans fitted into each other well" (Young, 66-67). The situation seemed ideal—as ideal as any situation could be in which Muir's perfect independence was not possible.

Nowhere in *Travels in Alaska*, or elsewhere, does Muir summarize his feelings about missionary work. It is doubtful that he could because there were simply too many variables in the equation. In the first place, he believed that the Indians themselves were only relatively better for their contact with the missionaries, and Muir was not even sure of that. "They beg for teachers and missionaries," he noted, "not probably because they are predisposed to piety, but simply because Christian teachers are the only ones they ever see" (*John of the Mountains*, 274-75). Muir recognized the Indians' need for some kind of betterment, if only to enable them to control their environment a little better; but he feared that they were exchanging their wildness for a civilized sterility. "It is too often found that in attempting to Christianize savages they become very nearly nothing, lose their wild instincts, and gain a hymnbook, without the means of living. . . . Then they mope and doze and die on the outskirts of civilization like tamed eagles in barn-yard corners, with blunt talons, blunt bills, and clipped wings" (275). The comparison is strikingly like that of "Wild Wool." Civilization "eats" the Indian just as it "eats" the sheep, under the guise of "reforming" in the one case, "domesticating" in the other.

Still, the missionaries are a relative good for the Indians, for without them the savages have no protection from the "whisky-laden traders" who represent a far greater evil. But the problem is never a simple one. The missionaries themselves are often less than perfect. Muir has nothing but contempt for the ecclesiastic member of one of the expeditions near Fort Wrangell who thoughtlessly cut down a Kadachan totem to take home "to enrich some museum or other." He pertinently includes a description of the man's discomfort at being asked by one of the Indians, "How would you like to have an Indian go into a graveyard and break down and carry away a monument belonging to your family?" (*Travels in Alaska*, 93).

On the whole, I think there can be little doubt that Muir believed that the Indians of Alaska in their state of nature were, relatively, closer to God than even the best of the missionaries who preached to them. It is only because their contact with civilization in its worst aspect was inevitable that he believed their conversion to Christianity had any value to them. Evidence of his attitude may best be seen in his long discussion of the Indians' understanding of the concept of atonement, which, he believed, was responsible for the "hearty welcome" the Thlingets gave to the Christian missionaries (240). He tells the story of a Stickeen chief who brought a great war with the Sitka tribe to an end by offering his own life in exchange for ten lives, this number being the difference in number of casualties of their war. "That chief literally gave himself [as] a sacrifice for his people," is Muir's comment on the incident. "Therefore, when missionaries preached the doctrine of atonement, explaining that when all mankind had gone astray, had broken God's laws and deserved to die, God's son came forward, and, like the Stickeen chief, offered himself as a sacrifice to heal the cause of God's wrath and set all the people of the world free, the doctrine was readily accepted" (242). These "savages," Muir is saying, have all the essentials of Christianity except the name. It is not the Stickeen chief who is like Christ, but Christ who is "like the Stickeen chief."

Throughout the account of the voyage of 1879 Muir balances what he considers "natural" goodness with doctrinal goodness—and always to the disadvantage of the latter. Perhaps the best example of the contrast is at the end of the description of his rescue of Young. When he finally succeeded in bringing Young down from the mountain where he had received his injury, the two men—both exhausted and hungry and Young crippled—waited at the gangplank of their steamer for help to get aboard. Several doctors of divinity and the captain of the vessel, Nat Lane, who "had been swearing in angry impatience" at having been kept waiting so long for Muir and Young to return, observed their approach. When Muir asked for help to get Young aboard, the doctors of divinity responded by reproaching Muir and Young. Young had no right to engage upon "foolish adventures" with Muir, "to risk your life on treacherous peaks and precipices," one of them harangued Young. Captain Lane was the only one to respond to Muir's call for help, "shouting in angry irreverence, 'Oh, blank! This is no time for preaching! Don't you see the man is hurt?'" (67-68).

Muir also provides a subtler contrast of moral positions in his description of his extensive travels with Young. At each village where they stop, Young speaks for many hours to the Indians, bringing the "Good News." But the Indians always want to hear from Muir, too, and so he is pressed to speak, each time delivering "a sort of lecture on the fine foodful country God had given them and the brotherhood of man" (208-9). Young's doctrine is received happily, but the Indians are more impressed with Muir's transcendence of it. One tribe asked

that Muir be sent as a missionary to them, and "as an induce-
ment, promised that if I would come to them they would always
do as I directed, follow my counsels, give me as many wives as
I liked, build a church and school, and pick all the stones out
of the paths and make them smooth for my feet" (210-11).

The matter is treated lightly, but its inclusion in the book is
suggestive. Muir must have believed that his own view of
religion was more attractive to these Indians than Young's, just
as his sympathies with them were more inclusive than those of
his young clerical companion. His alliance with Young was
possible because of the sweet goodness of the missionary, not
at all because of any sympathy on Muir's part for the doctrine
he preached. One cannot but wish that either Muir or Young
had reproduced in his account a more complete summary of
the talks Muir made to these Indians. I have no doubt that they
were of a character that would have embarrassed a missionary
less receptive than Young to the unorthodoxies in which Muir
believed.

III *Stickeen*

Muir's second trip to Alaska in 1880, after his marriage, was a
kind of bachelor's holiday. Muir and his wife agreed that the
period between July and October, while the fruits of their farm
were ripening, "should be his each year for a trip to the
wilderness."[4] In 1880 Muir returned to Alaska to rediscover the
glacier by Sum Dum Bay that he had been forced to leave behind in 1879 because of the advancing winter season. His few
months among the mountains and glaciers in 1880 were then
very similar to the explorations made in 1879. There was one
exception, however: the presence of the dog, Stickeen.

I do not share in the boundless admiration which Muir's
biographers have showered on his most famous story, *Stickeen*.
One called it "one of the greatest dog stories ever written," another that it "ranks with 'Rab and His Friends,' 'Bob, Son of
Battle,' and far above 'The Call of the Wild.'"[5] Now, all that
may very possibly be true, but still does not say much for the
story. On any rational scale of excellence, *Stickeen* must rank
very low in comparison with practically any of Muir's more
thoughtful works. One can see that it was inevitable that Muir
would write such a story sometime in his life. He certainly had
the requisite feelings toward animals and surely was bound at
one time or another to encounter just such a dog—or cat, or

trained badger, or coatamundi—that would produce a *Stickeen.* To me, the phenomenon itself, the story, is far less interesting than the complex of personality and desires which went into the making of it.

A part of the anti-anthropocentrism that was so important in the development of Muir's mature philosophy and was evident in his writings as early as 1867 was the belief in non-human sentience. Examples of it are rife in Muir's work, and *Travels in Alaska* is no exception, even excluding the anecdote of Stickeen. Muir quoted with approbation the Indian belief that wild birds communicate during their migrations. He "greatly enjoyed" their discussion over a campfire about the language of animals, their wisdom, and their position in the afterlife, with which he certainly agreed more completely than he did with the orthodox Christian view (150-52).

Usually in Muir's writings animals have an important place and fulfill functions important to his themes and ideas. The amorous adventures of Shepherd Billy's dog Jack, in *My First Summer in the Sierra* (61-63), provide a minor but effective counterpoint to the central theme of the opposition of culture and nature in that book. Muir's observations on sheep, the water ouzel of California, the Douglas squirrel, and many other animals are all important and effective supplements to his purposes in writing.

The key word is "supplements." In none of these instances is the "cuteness" of an animal reported for its own sake. To do so is to approach dangerously close to sentimentality. Muir seems to approach the sentimental many times, but he almost always keeps clear. In each case there is a further purpose in mind to which the incident recorded is subordinate. Now, Muir had a natural tendency toward sentimentality in his personal life. Young has recorded how Muir botanized in the fields of Alaska with a mixture of scientific language and baby talk: "'Ah! my blue-eyed darlin', little did I think to see you here. How did you stray away from Shasta?'

"'Well, well! Who'd 'a' thought that you'd have left that niche in the Merced Mountains to come here!'

"'And who might you be, now, with your wonder look? Is it possible that you can be (two Latin polysyllables)? You're lost, my dear; you belong in Tennessee'" (Young, 20). While that sort of diction is not entirely absent from his writings, it is striking, on the whole, how little of it Muir allowed in print.

He was a dedicated and conscious professional as a writer and recognized the dangers of sentimentality.

Why, then, did he publish *Stickeen* at all? First, of course, because he was greatly moved by the incident. Young described how, contrary to his usual volubility after an adventure, Muir returned from the escapade with Stickeen to sit quietly for some time before he began to tell what happened, prefacing the story simply and movingly with the comment, "Yon's a brave doggie" (185). Furthermore, he believed strongly in the intelligence of animals and wished, by quoting the specific example of Stickeen, to stress the general concept. And finally, he must have been eager to use an anecdote in which the heroism of another simple natural creature took the emphasis away from himself, a persistent problem which he faced throughout his life. As it was, Muir worked over the story for seventeen years, filling a whole notebook with unsuccessful efforts, before he published the 1897 version of *Stickeen*. And he was not satisfied with his efforts even then. When he came to retell the incident in *Travels in Alaska*, he shortened and simplified it considerably, leaving out much of the "humanizing" of the dog (309-11). Torn between a very human desire and his artistic discipline, he gave into the desire; but not without much labor and many misgivings over the whole affair.

IV *In the Ice Pack*

Muir's Alaska trip of 1880, the shortest and the most confined of the five, lasted only two months and was restricted to a small area on the southern coast of Alaska. When, next year, he was invited by Captain C. L. Hooper of the *Corwin* to participate in a much more extensive Alaska voyage, he at first refused, as a good married man must, and then, after talking the matter over with his wife, accepted. The *Corwin* was to cruise in far northern waters on an extensive search for clues about the fate of the *Jeannette,* which had disappeared in 1879. But the cruise was also to be a scientific expedition. Mr. E. W. Nelson, of the Smithsonian Institute, was to examine things archaeological and zoological; Muir was to study the geological and botanical curiosities of the Far North.

The result, in terms of Muir's writings, was a series of letters published in the San Francisco *Evening Bulletin* and two scientific articles—"Botanical Notes," on the flora of Herald Island and Wrangell Land and some other areas of Siberia and Alaska; and "The Glaciation of the Arctic and Sub-Arctic Regions Visited During the Cruise of the *Corwin*," both of which were published as government documents. When William F. Badé edited the Sierra Edition of Muir's works, he used the *Bulletin* letters as the basis for Volume VII, *The Cruise of the Corwin*; but he supplemented the letters with Muir's journals and republished the two scientific papers as an appendix to the volume.

The Cruise of the Corwin is at once the most exotic and the least Transcendental of Muir's writings. It is, of all his books, the one closest to being a simple travelogue; exciting in its descriptions of strange places and people, it rarely rises to the level of philosophic comment so often found in the descriptions of his California travels. One reason for this is the fact that the original articles were intended for newspaper publication, a form not too well suited for heights of rhetoric or reflection. But Muir had overcome like obstacles with his California writings, and could have done so with this material if that were the only problem. The fact is that both the material observed and the condition of the observer were not such as to lead to much more than superficial observations. Muir was ever a tourist in Alaska, and could never achieve the familiarity with his subject matter necessary for the kind of reflection which is so striking in his California works. Furthermore, the exotic nature of the Alaskan and Siberian climate and people is so interesting in itself that pure, straightforward reporting seems the only possible technique.

His motives for taking part in the expedition are also important in relation to the success of his writing. Muir's purpose in accepting Hooper's invitation was almost entirely scientific. He went "to read the ice record" of the islands and coast of the Bering Sea as a continuation of his interest in glacial action.[6] But, where his interest in California glaciers became philosophically involved in the concept of flow in nature and the continuous production of landscape beauty, his studies in Alaska were more practical. He hoped, primarily, to support his earlier conclusions about glaciers by observing, as if with a controlled experiment in a laboratory, the effects of extensive glacial action taking place in the present. Yosemite was formed—everchanging, to be sure, but a beautiful *result* of the natural processes of glaciation. Alaska was still in the process of becoming. Muir's trips to Alaska might be likened to the situation of an artist who deeply loves the human form and who, for better knowledge of it, studies preserved foetuses and attends a birth. Neither observation is likely to produce artistic work of itself, but both may be necessary for a full realization of the finished form.

Still, *The Cruise of the Corwin* is one of Muir's most exciting works. It reads, in places, like a suspense novel. Will the *Corwin* find evidence of the lost *Jeannette*? Or will it become trapped in the ice itself, subjecting the crew and Muir to the rigors of shipwreck in that unwelcoming climate? Nature in this book, strange paradox, is the antagonist of the efforts of man, at least insofar as the book is a narration of shipwreck and disaster. The chapter titles alone suggest this theme: "In Peril from the Pack," "Approaching a Mysterious Land," "Tragedies of the Whaling Fleet," and "Turned Back by Storms and Ice." Muir, partly because of the ephemeral newspaper publication of his letters, makes full use of the sheer adventure of the voyage. And he is quite right to do so, for peril accompanies every chapter of the book in a way that it does not in any other of his writings.

Accompanying the theme of suspense are several other themes which are more familiar in Muir's writings. Just as in *Travels in Alaska* he found the Alaska Indians to be a people worthy of their wild existence, so in this book does he find the Aleuts, the Chukchis of Siberia, and the Eskimos of Alaska. But even here, in Muir's common theme of the dignity of wildness, is the aspect of the tourist. He discusses the people of Alaska and Siberia as much as phenomena as rightful inhabitants of the wilderness. The Aleuts of Unalaska can earn "from four hundred to eight hundred dollars per annum" as hunters, but are declining in population (14). The Aleuts of St. Paul are in a unique situation, since they are entirely under the white control, working as butchers for the Alaska Commercial Company (19). Comparisons of features and religions among the various tribes draw comments from Muir: "The Chukchis are taller and more resolute-looking people than the Eskimos of the opposite coast" (46). "Shamanism with slight variation extends over all Siberia and Alaska" (18). Such matters of fact are found in all of Muir's books, but they are predominant in this one alone.

Muir does not eschew comparison between wild freedom and tame bondage in this book, however much of the travelogue he includes. The Eskimos are "better behaved than white men, not half so greedy, shameless, or dishonest." An Eskimo baby is happier than any that "could be found in warm parlors, where loving attendants anticipate every want and the looms of the world afford their best in the way of soft fabrics" (75). Even a half-European girl raised in an Eskimo family is "plump, red-cheeked, and in every way a picture of health . . . beautiful, well-behaved, happy and healthy," a fact which is to Muir "very notable" (81).

As usual, when he makes comparisons between the vices of wildness and those of civilization, he is inclined to favor wildness: "Though savage and sensual [the Eskimos] are by no means dull or apathetic like the sensual savages of civilization, who live only to eat and indulge the senses" (142).

Muir's greatest praise is for the esthetic of the Eskimos. Their living quarters, more keyed to their natural surroundings than those of whites, are preferable. The Aleuts of Western Diomede Island have summer houses made of walrus skins stretched over poles which are "the queerest human nests conceivable," but admirable in their simplicity and naturalness. "The entire establishment is window, one pane for the roof, which is also the ceiling, and one for each of the four sides, without cross sash-bars to mar the brave simplicity of it all" (237). The huts of the Unalaska Aleuts are even more natural and picturesque in the late summer. "The grass grows tall over the sides and the roof, waving in the wind, and making a fine fringe about the windows and the door" (250). Such dwellings are not close to nature, but a part of nature itself.

Civilization is fast encroaching upon even this far-removed haven of naturalness. The Eskimos are able to trade ivory, seals, and whalebone with the whites and are becoming dependent upon this trade, losing many of their native skills. They "obtain more of the white man's goods than is well used. They probably were better off before they were possessed of a single civilized blessing—so many are the evils accompanying them" (70). Chief of these evils is, of course, alcohol. Muir does not go into the causes of the Eskimo's craving for alcohol, but he does thoroughly explore its effects: "To the Eskimo [alcohol] is misery and often-times quick death. Two years ago the inhabitants of several villages on this island died of starvation caused by abundance of rum, which rendered them careless about the laying up of ordinary supplies of food for the winter. Then an unusually severe season followed, bringing famine, and, after eating their dogs, they lay down and died in their huts" (27).

The effects of civilization are the more vicious upon the Eskimos because their existence in the inhospitable Arctic is so tenuous. Muir must look to animals to find inhabitants that are truly at home here. He describes the raucous discomfort of the sled dogs aboard the *Corwin* and their pleasure at being released from the ship: "When the dogs got upon the ice, their native heath, they rolled and raced about in exuberant sport. The rough pack was home, sweet home to them, though a more forbidding combination of rough water, ice, and driving snow could hardly be imagined by the sunny civilized south" (52). The dogs, and the other animals of the North, are the only creatures capable of living in true harmony with this wildest of natural surroundings. Reindeer have a fine wool fur which enables "the animal to resist the keenest frosts of the Arctic winter without any shelter beyond the lee side of a rock or hill" (233). The dogs, which are really only barely tamed wolves, have the same capacity. The walrus and seal seem wonderful to Muir with their capacity to "live happily enough to grow fat and keep full of warm red blood with water at 32° F. for [their] pasture field, and wet sludge for [their] bed" (24-25). But polar bears are to Muir "the unrivaled master-existence of this ice-bound solitude," the most perfectly adapted to life in the Arctic.

The adaptation of these animals to their circumstances excites Muir's admiration completely. His esteem for the Eskimos is also aroused by their capacity for adaptation to the climate in which they live. The influence of trade upon them, quite apart from the deleterious effect of their dependence upon whisky and kvass, which are to Muir only the worst of a host of civilized evils, is debilitating. Muir uses the situation as a means of criticizing the excesses of civilized society. When some of the members of the *Corwin* expedition, "fun-, fur-, and fame-seekers," succeed in shooting three polar bears from the hardly sportsmanlike advantage of the deck of the steamer, he remarks that the affair "was as safe and easy a butchery as shooting cows in a barnyard from the roof of the barn. It was prolonged, bloody agony, as clumsily and heartlessly inflicted as it could well be" (176). He contrasts this incident with the bear hunts of the Eskimos: "The Eskimos hunt and kill [polar bears] for food, going out to meet them on the ice with spears and dogs. This is merely one savage living on another. But how civilized people, seeking for heavens and angels and millenniums, and the reign of universal peace and love, can enjoy this red, brutal amusement, is not so easily accounted for" (176).

The Eskimos, "savages living on other savages," are to be commended for their understanding and respect of the rights of such wild animals as the polar bear, "the master-existence" of the Arctic. But civilized man as a hunter of "commodity" has no such respect. He kills walruses "for their tusks alone, like buffaloes for their tongues, ostriches for their feathers, or for mere sport and exercise. In nothing does man, with his grand notions of heaven and charity, show forth his innate, low-bred, wild animalism more clearly than in his treatment of his brother beasts. From the shepherd with his lambs to the red-handed hunter, it is the same; no recognition of rights—only murder in one form or another" (156). As can be seen from this comment, the word "savage" in Muir's writing is not necessarily derogatory. The savage often acts bravely and naturally; it is the civilized being who acts in a corrupt and disgusting manner.

Indeed, a scale of righteousness of existence may be deduced from this book, a scale which reads like a reversal of the great chain of being. At the head of it are the polar bears and walruses and seals, living an honest natural life, feeding and being fed upon, and procreating at a rate suitable for continued existence. Beneath these on the scale are the native Eskimos, also feeding and being fed upon, but less well adapted to life in the Arctic, and in some measure unfitted to the perpetuity of the chain. For the Eskimos "make it a rule to kill every animal that comes within reach, without a thought of future scarcity, fearing, as some say, that, should they refuse to kill as opportunity offers, though it be at a time when food is no object, then the deer-spirit would be offended at the refusal of his gifts and would not send any deer when they are in want. Probably, however, they are moved simply by an instinctive love of killing on which their existence depends, and these wholesale slaughters are to be regarded as only too much of a good thing" (139-40). They are, like all humans, thoughtless and governed by needs beyond survival, whether it be blood lust or religion, and therefore are less perfect than the polar bears.

But their imperfections are worsened by the lowest group in the scale, the "civilized" man who upsets all the balances, giving the Eskimos rifles so that their capacity for slaughter is increased a hundredfold, and wreaking their own evils upon the precarious balance of nature in the Arctic. Like the shepherd in "Wild Wool," they are engaged upon a process of "eating" every inhabitant of the Arctic, by reducing the functions of each to some place in the white man's scheme of the commercial values of nature. It is a grim picture that Muir paints, and it is lightened hardly at all. One of the few extenuations of the circumstances given by Muir in this book is his description of the prospects of P. H. Ray's Point Barrow expedition of 1881-83. Here is, Muir feels, an opportunity for civilized man to live within the balance of nature and perhaps to learn from it. "At first sight," he begins, "it would seem a gloomy time to look forward to—three years in so remote and so severely desolate and forbidding a region, generally regarded as the top-most, frostkilled end of creation! But, amid all the disadvantages of position, these men have much in their lot for which they might well be envied by people dwelling in softer climates." After they have had their opportunity to "study the habits of the reindeer on the tundras and the magnificent polar bear among the ice—the master animal of the north," they will perceive something which the hunters commuting from the south will never know, and will perhaps help to restore the lost balance (219).

Here is the central concept of *The Cruise of the Corwin*: Adaptation to nature produces life, destruction of the balance of nature produces death. Though the theme is not developed coherently or even explicitly in the book, Muir points it out through the use of a series of images which belong to poetry, and which make parts of the book a kind of epic. No part of Muir's writing is better known than his descriptions of the "villages of the dead" in Alaska, yet no one seems to have noticed how pointed those descriptions are toward the significance of the theme of life and the balance of nature. The description of the several hundred Eskimos who died on Tapkan Island as a result of improvidence fostered by alcohol is one example of an externally produced imbalance in nature. But it is only one example, and the several other instances given in the book support and amplify it thematically. The descriptions of these annihilated villages are haunting and poetic, as Muir intended them to be; but his purpose did not end with the production of a mood in the reader. Each example contributes to the dominant motif of the relationship between life, death, and the balance of nature.

Muir began to set up the image-contrast early in the book with his description of the Tapkan Island deaths. He then continued with a description of a second nearly annihilated village on St. Lawrence Island. Here for the first time he used a technique of contrast. The macabre scene is described and counterpointed by the attitudes of several of the survivors. When Muir and the others from the *Corwin* ask what has happened, the Eskimos smile continuously as they explain, "All mucky." "All gone." "Dead?" "Yes, dead!" They continue to smile "at the ghastly spectacle of the grinning skulls and bleached bones appearing through the brown, shrunken skin" of the corpses which cannot be buried in the frozen Arctic ground (94). The causes and conditions of this second "village of the dead" are left enigmatic in Muir's account. The resolution of both theme and action must wait until the third, climactic encounter with catastrophic death in the Arctic, in which Muir used the presence of E. W. Nelson and his Smithsonian collection as a final contrasting symbol to point his thematic moral.

Nelson, under Muir's literary hands, becomes an unconscious archetype of the forces producing unbalance in nature. When the expedition arrives at the next Eskimo "cemetery," a corpse-strewn area of ground, Nelson is left "alone in his glory" by Muir to despoil the corpses of "ivory spears, arrows, dishes of various kinds, and a stone hammer," which "formed the least ghastly of his spoils." Muir, on the other hand, "pushed to the top of the divide, then followed it westward to the highest summit on the peninsula, whence I obtained the views I was in search of" (112). The lengthy and lyric description of the view thus made available to him is in direct contrast to Nelson's "ghastly" occupation. To point the contrast more clearly, Muir adds at the end of the narrative that "when the natives saw Mr. Nelson returning without me they said that he had killed me" (113). Nelson is, in all these descriptions, everywhere associated with death; Muir, in his search for beautiful natural landscapes, is always contrasted with him.

The climax occurs when the expedition returns to another shore of St. Lawrence Island. Once again Nelson is prominent in his archetypal role. At St. Michael he obtains "a lot of skulls and specimens of one sort and another," and at a larger village down the shore he and Muir together view the most grisly sight of desolation yet encountered.

> We found twelve desolate huts close to the beach with about two hundred skeletons in them or strewn about on the rocks and rubbish heaps within a few yards of the doors. The scene was indescribably ghastly and desolate, though laid in a country purified by frost as by fire. Gulls, plovers, and ducks were swimming and flying about in happy life, the pure salt sea was dashing white against the shore, the blooming tundra swept back to the snow-clad volcanoes, and the wide azure sky bent kindly over all—nature intensely fresh and sweet, the village lying in the foulest and most glaring death.   (119-20)

To this explicit contrast in description, Muir adds the implicit contrast of the figures of his narrative. Nelson "went into this Golgotha with hearty enthusiasm, gathering the fine white harvest of skulls spread before him, and throwing them in heaps like a boy gathering pumpkins" (121).

The final stroke of the contrast returns the narrative to the feelings of the natives. A survivor, when asked what happened to the rest of his village, "answered with a happy, heedless smile, 'All mucky.' 'All gone!' 'Dead?' 'Yes, dead, all dead!'"—recapitulating the earlier experience with similar words. "Then he led us a few yards back of his hut and pointed to twelve or fourteen skeletons lying on the brown grass, repeating in almost a merry tone of voice, 'Dead, yes, all dead, all mucky, all gone!'" (122).

Three points of view are here identified with three characters intended to be types or emblems of human relationships to nature. The Eskimos who speak to Nelson and Muir represent the closest identification with the balance of nature. They smile and speak "merrily" of the scenes of death because it is to them a natural process and, furthermore, one by which they profit, since it improves the balance of nature in their favor.[7] In direct contrast to the merriment of the Eskimos is Nelson's hideous glee at the "specimens" which these catastrophes have afforded him. Although Muir unquestionably recognized the scientific validity of Nelson's researches, to Muir Nelson is still an "outsider" to nature and the natural considerations of this phenomenon of wholesale death in the Arctic. Nelson's science is totally external; it is bound up in museums and collections of dead things. Muir's is, of course, exactly the opposite.

As for Muir himself, the third figure of this little allegory, he is sympathetic to the processes of nature and to the plight of the Eskimos. The old balance of nature obviously can never be restored, but Muir is not very certain about what can take its place. His summary paragraph about the situation is curiously indirect: "About two hundred perished here, and unless some aid be extended by our government which claims these people, in a few years at most every soul of them will have vanished from the face of the earth; for, even when alcohol is left out of the count, the few articles of food, clothing, guns, etc., furnished by the traders, exert a degrading influence, making them less self-reliant, and less skillful as hunters. They seem easily susceptible of civilization, and well deserve the attention of our government" (122). That is, a return to the old situation no longer being possible, Muir urges that the government complete the process of civilization for the Eskimos, taking them out of the balance of nature in their environment entirely. Nobody who has read any of Muir's other books could possibly believe that this solution seems ideal to him; but, the degradation of the Eskimos having become an accomplished fact, he can see no other course of action possible.

V *Final Journeys*

Muir traveled twice more to Alaska. In 1890, to combat a bout of sickness with his own peculiar panacea—a regimen of ice and snow—he spent several months on and about Muir Glacier. His description of that period, the last, unfinished, segment of *Travels in Alaska,* is full of horrendous situations, the more impressive when one considers that Muir was then fifty-two years old. He got rid of the cold, since "no lowland microbe could stand such a trip" (355); but he suffered from a slip into a water-filled crevasse, from snow-blindness, and from other assorted perils. The narration in *Travels in Alaska* is in a rather rough form, and probably would have been revised considerably had Muir lived longer.

Not included in the volume is Muir's final Alaska venture, the Harriman expedition of 1899. Muir's journals of the trip have been published in *John of the Mountains,* however, and present a charming view of the rather plush expedition (the steamship *George W. Elder* was fitted out as a floating laboratory for the benefit of the scientists aboard). The account includes a good deal of the raillery between John Burroughs and Muir, capped by Muir's fine doggerel account of Burrough's seasickness in the Bering Sea. It was really the final word in an exchange of doggerel, for Burroughs had written much uncomplimentary verse about Muir's part in luring him into this final phase of the expedition. As a war of wits, it ended about in a draw, although Muir did have the last word.

Muir's life after 1900 was spent in revising journals and periodical writings for publication in permanent form. He continued his work for national parks, in particular for the recession of the California controlled section of Yosemite to the federal government, which was finally accomplished in 1905. He was not so fortunate in his efforts to save the Hetch Hetchy Valley from exploiters who wanted to tap its water supply for San Francisco. But that one disappointment was offset by countless honors received during his last years. He expanded his knowledge of his home on "Earth-planet, Universe," with trips to South America, Africa, and Europe while en route around the world. These travels have no place in his writing, however. He died of pneumonia in Los Angeles on December 24, 1914.

CHAPTER 6

Apostle of Nature

IT SEEMS LIKELY that Muir will never be very widely *studied* as a writer. Who can imagine a college course in which Emerson and Thoreau are the subject for the first semester and Muir for the second? The imbalance of such an arrangement is ridiculous, and yet, in terms of variety of experience, sheer quantity of life spent in nature, and breadth, if not depth, of description, Muir is certainly a more extensive "subject" than Thoreau, and quite out of Emerson's league entirely. No, it is in terms of literary quality, not experiential quantity, that we arrange our college courses, and a good thing that is, too. Furthermore, in two other areas important to curriculum committees Muir is deficient: influence upon later writers and sheer difficulty of style. Emerson's position as a fountainhead of an American doctrine that stretches all the way from Concord to the present is just now beginning to be fully appreciated. And Thoreau, since the advent of New Criticism, is often beatified for his difficulty alone. Muir, on the other hand, had little literary influence beyond that exerted upon formula writers for magazines like *Field and Stream* and nice old ladies who write epistles to newspapers about what the new highway is doing to the loveliest field of daisies in the state. And his writings seem so simple and straightforward (though I hope this book has shown that judgment to be something of a misconception) that the word *study* when applied to them seems inappropriate.

If he will not be studied, Muir will nevertheless continue to be read. His less enduring monuments—Muir Glacier, Muir Woods, and the many other places that bear his name—are the kind of temples which inspire their worshipers to a deeper knowledge. Some of these admirers will always go to the writings of the man thus naturally recommended to them. Few, I suspect, will be willing to accept the philosophy implicit in his writings, even among those who understand it. It is an idealism less adaptable to the modern world than was even Emerson's. Emerson has been made palatable to the modern taste by a debasement of his spiritual idealism to serve the ends of a mushrooming commercial society. About all that is left of Emerson is his optimism, and, oh, what ends that is made to serve. Could he return to see what valedictory context he is quoted in about hitching wagons to stars, he would never rest quiet again.

But, though Muir's ideas too are debased through the modern industry of tourism,[1] he has left too many outspoken evidences of his peculiar kind of spirituality to suffer exactly the same fate as Emerson. Though he may be quoted and misquoted in Kodacolor illustrated brochures, he will have the pleasure of knowing that some parts of the wilderness he loved may yet work upon the poor tourists who are lured there, that "they will forget themselves and become devout." Those who are willing to read him carefully will find what the brochures never include.

His significance in American literature is a result of three elements of his writing. In order of importance they are: first, his achievement as a scientist; second, the quality of his prose; and third, his philosophy, especially in relation to the mainstream of American Transcendentalism. To arrive at a final clear view of his position, it is first necessary to examine coherently some aspects of material which I have touched upon often during the last five chapters as it relates to these three topics.

I *The Base of the Pyramid*

To be believable, the writings of any idealist must be based on such a solid foundation of fact that the higher flights of his imagination do not shock the reader out of sympathy. Muir's scientific observations serve this purpose for his philosophic observations. Just as Melville bound his most intense speculation about man's position in the universe to the processes of whaling, and Thoreau to the problems of logistics and economy on the shores of a very real Walden Pond, so Muir's effectiveness as a writer depends upon the accuracy of his observations on glaciers, the formation of mountains, the presence in a specific field of a specific growth of cassiope.

Muir poses as a scientist in much of his writing, seeming to be interested in recording the phenomena themselves, but actually his purposes far transcend simple observation. A good example of his use of this technique is his commentary on the Yosemite or Inyo earthquake of 1872. What more terrifying phenomenon of nature could Muir describe than an earthquake? And yet, in his description it becomes just another example, the most extreme perhaps, of the orderliness of the processes of nature. His attempt to show that earthquakes are indeed orderly and a part of the flow of nature shocks our belief in him immediately. Who could believe, unsupported by some scientific evidence, a statement about the results of an earthquake that reads: "on the whole, by what at first sight seemed pure confusion and ruin, the landscape was enriched"? Muir then seeks to restore the reader's faith in him by presenting scientific proofs of two kinds: apparent objective proof of his statement, and reassuringly sober description of his scientific means of evaluation.

Muir is *posing* as a scientist when he offers in support of his beliefs about earthquakes what appears to be an objective test:

> If for a moment you are inclined to regard these taluses [sloping fields of broken rock] as mere draggled, chaotic dumps, climb to the top of one of them, tie your mountain shoes firmly over the instep, and with braced nerves run down without any haggling, puttering hesitation, boldly jumping from boulder to boulder with even speed. You will then find your feet playing a tune, and quickly discover the music and poetry of rock piles,—a fine lesson; and all nature's wildness tells the same story. Storms of every sort, torrents, earthquakes, cataclysms, "convulsions of nature," etc., however mysterious and lawless at first sight they may seem, are only harmonious notes in the song of creation, varied expressions of God's love.
>
> (*Our National Parks*, 289)

As a scientific test, this careering course down a talus slope leaves something to be desired. It has the advantage to Muir's argument of being the kind of experiment that only a sympathetic reader would try, and one in which sympathy with the theory becomes a necessity for the success of the experiment. Any halting "careful" efforts at running down talus slopes are likely to end in crumpled, bruised heaps at the bottom. No, this kind of validation of Muir's observations could hardly be called scientific. It smacks more of oriental passive acceptance, of a Buddhist or Zen miracle. The reader cries for more positive support, and Muir gives it.

In comparison with the total description of the earthquake, Muir's discussion of his scientific observations are brief, but the dispassionate wording of this part of his description is reassuring far beyond its length. After relating several anecdotes in which he ridicules the fears of others who are observing the earthquake, Muir set to his scientific work. "The rocks trembled more or less every day for over two months, and I kept a bucket of water on my table to learn what I could of the movements. The blunt thundertones in the depths of the mountains were usually followed by sudden jarring, horizontal thrusts from the northward, often succeeded by twisting, upjolting movements" (287-88). Not much description here, but the matter-of-fact rhetoric, combined with a show of scientific tools, is very reassuring for it objectivity. A bucket of water is still a usable piece of equipment for a seismologist, and the accuracy of Muir's objective recording of the character of earth movements helps to make the reader accept his transcendence of scientific observation to the assertion that even such apparent cataclysms exhibit the characteristics of an orderly process.

Muir uses science in this way throughout his writings. For all I know, his observations may have great scientific validity,[2] but, as they appear in his writings, their main purpose is to support his less scientific ideas about order, harmony, and the constant flow in nature. His two principal areas of scientific investigation and achievement, botany and geology, are peculiarly suited to his purposes. In his hands, they are tools by which he can explain the concepts of the eternity of creation and the integrity of each individual creature, presenting what seems to be a laboratory analysis of Emerson's unity in diversity.

Botany, Muir's first love, was always for him a key to something more than an arbitrary classification of plants. Instead, he saw it as a tool for probing the inner beauty of the plant kingdom, "revealing glorious traces of the thoughts of God, and leading on and on into the infinite cosmos" (*Boyhood and Youth*, 225). Young, accompanying Muir on several botanical expeditions, discovered that Muir's botanizing was intended less as scientific investigation than as "spiritual insight into Nature's lore" (*Alaska Days with John Muir*, 21). For Muir, no finer proof of God existed than the ordering of an infinity of forms into relationships of species and genuses. That the pea and the locust, so different in externals, could be of the same family was a revelation. The botanist, through a study of the diversity of creation, comes inevitably to the realization that underlying it all is a harmonious unity.

Muir's geology was similarly limited. He had little interest in the processes of mountain creation, simply because such creation was unmeasurable in terms of time. Was it the work of a few instants, or of long periods of gradual upheaval? Muir could not tell for certain, though his observations on the order and harmony of the Yosemite earthquake of 1872, quoted above, show his opinions on that subject. The creation of landscape as an eternal process was his great interest, and the mightiest force in such an eternal creation was, for the mountains of California and the coastline of Alaska, the glacier. Thus he became an expert on glaciation. His scientific achievement in this area is considerable, but, again, it is unquestionably subordinate to the spiritual values he assigned to the processes of glaciation. Most geologists would agree that the "Studies in the Sierra" are a fine piece of work sustained with but little of the technical equipment available to modern geologists. Muir seems to have been the first geologist to have interpreted accurately the means of formation of kettle moraines, a minor but significant contribution to that science.[3] His observations on glacial flow, the production of moraines, contours of the carvings of glaciers, and the like make *Travels in Alaska* and *The Cruise of the Corwin* adequate introductory texts to the study of glacial action.

Muir was a competent scientific observer, both as a botanist and as a geologist. But it is the very limitations of his scientific studies that have made him a fine writer. He could not confine his observations of the twining lily (*stropholorion Californicum*) to a notation of its location and class; he had to add this comment: "like most other things not apparently useful to man, it has few friends, and the blind question, 'Why was it made?' goes on and on with never a guess that first of all it might have been made for itself" (*My First Summer*, 26). Or, a full botanical description of the silver pine provokes this comment: "were [stands of silver pine] mere mechanical sculptures, what noble objects they would still be! How much more throbbing, thrilling, overflowing, full of life in every fiber and cell, grand glowing silver rods—the very gods of the plant kingdom, living their sublime century lives in sight of Heaven, watched and loved and admired from generation to generation!" (*My First Summer*, 52). And, though his glacial observations be accurate, they are subordinate to his ideas about the planning and purpose of landscape, and, above all, the eternity of creation:

> Standing here, with facts so fresh and telling and held up so vividly before us, every seeing observer, not to say geologist, must readily apprehend the earth-sculpturing, landscape-making action of flowing ice. And here, too, one learns that the world, though made, is yet being made; that this is still the morning of creation; that mountains long conceived are now being born, channels traced for coming rivers, basins hollowed for lakes; that moraine soil is being ground and outspread for coming plants,—coarse boulders and gravel for forests, finer soil for grasses and flowers,—while the finest part of the grist, seen hastening out to sea in the draining streams, is being stored away in darkness and builded particle on particle, cementing and crystallizing, to make the mountains and valleys and plains of other predestined landscapes, to be followed by still others in endless rhythm and beauty. (*Travels in Alaska*, 84-85)

II *The Noble Blotting of Glorious Lines*

Nobody can read very far in Muir without discovering what his greatest rhetorical flaw is. One sometimes groans aloud at encountering the third or fourth "glorious" in a paragraph, then discovers on the very next page a paragraph similarly composed of excess "nobles." Muir was aware of the fault and worked to rid his manuscripts of superfluous "gloriouses,"[4] but one sometimes feels that he accomplished his purpose by substituting "nobles" for "gloriouses" and vice versa. His style is marred by overuse of adjectives generally, a fault hard to avoid in writing that is necessarily descriptive. If he never succeeded in overcoming the fault, he was always aware of it and tried to keep it to a minimum in his best writings.

Muir was always a self-conscious artist in prose. That fact, however opposed to the cliché of the Transcendental writer, is inescapable. He labored over his writing. He was "never satisfied with a sentence until it balanced well. [He] . . . had the keenest sense of melody, as well as of harmony, in his sentence structure" (Young, *Alaska Days*, 188). Muir's voluminous journals reveal any number of times his consciousness of the difficulty of transforming a physical action or phenomenon into a written description of the same thing. He always recognized that description inevitably falsified the original experience. Whether described adjectivally, metaphorically, or realistically, the beauty of a fact of nature defied perfect description. Muir has left dozens of examples testifying to his search for perfection.

One passage in his journals will serve as evidence of his self-conscious artistry in this respect. Struck by the beauty of the falls of Yosemite one day, he attempted three different descriptions, each using a different technique. First, a combination of his own sense impressions with a baroque metaphor:

> Today the falls were in terrible power. I gazed upon the mighty torrent of snowy, cometized water, whether in or out of the body I can hardly tell—such overwhelming displays of power and beauty almost bring the life out of our feeble tabernacle. I shouted until I was exhausted and sore with excitement. Down came the infuriate waters chafed among the combative buttresses of unflinching granite until they roared like ten thousand furies, screaming, hissing, surging like the maddened onset of all the wild spirits of the mountain sky—a perfect hell of conflicting demons.

This experiment in a reversal of the pathetic fallacy gives way in the next paragraph to a disclaimer and a renewed attempt, this time toward idealism and a hyperbolic metaphor: "But I speak after the manner of men, for there was no look or syllable of fury among all the songs and gestures of these living waters. No thought of war, no complaining discord, not the faintest breath of confusion. One stupendous unit of light and song, perfect and harmonious as any in heaven." Sensing that his earlier description had violated the concept of harmony which he felt was integral to the falls, Muir reacts here to the opposite extreme, minimizing his own feeling of sublimity to stress the order of the spectacle.

But that was not adequate either, for it gave no idea of the form of the falls, only the sensation of harmony. Muir next attempted a catalog and natural description, but eventually resorted again to metaphor:

> This gathering of mountain water, on reaching this Yosemite portion of their lives, is carefully prepared for this rock display and rock music. Before reaching the brow of their falls, they are deflected from side to side upon granite instruments of proper angle [compare, "combative buttresses of unflinching granite," above], whirled and gurgled in eddies and potholes, carefully mixed with measured portions of air, calmed in pool basins, and finally moved over the brink with songs that go farther into the

substance of our being than ever was touched by man-made harmonies—songs that bear pure heaven in every note. The fleecy, spiritualized waters take the form of mashed and woven comets, going with a grace that casts poor mortals into an agony of joy.   (*John of the Mountains*, 43)

After turning the description every way possible, Muir ends with an emphasis on the predestination of the waters toward beauty, and a return to his own feelings.

Such intense efforts to solve the problems of converting experience to communication are not rare in Muir's journals as I have shown in Chapter 4. He was fully conscious of the problem and worked conscientiously to overcome it. In the example just quoted, the first and last descriptions are totally different in their effect upon the reader, but both are essentially poetic in that they appeal primarily not to the sensations but to the emotion of the reader. The first, Muir recognized, falsified the experience by exaggerating the emotion of the spectator. The last, by use of the device of *apparently* suggesting the detailed, orderly process of movement of the water, makes the emotion of the spectator, now reduced to the simple "agony of joy," both more intense and more believable.

Usually Muir improved upon his first impression of a scene in nature in later versions of the same description. His journals are fountains for his more polished work no less than the mountains were to him fountains for the beauty of streams and glaciers. One can find many examples in *John of the Mountains* of the first recording of experiences which were later improved by changes, often of matters of fact, for later publication. There is no better example than the events of the evening of April 3, 1871, which were described by Muir no less than three times, each time more effectively.[5] A comparison of these three forms shows vividly how Muir revised his writings, changing emphasis and even factual details for effects.

Taking advantage of a moonlit night, Muir was observing the Falls of the Yosemite from Fern Ledge, alongside the falls and partway up. He noticed a narrow ledge leading behind the spray of water and determined to take the opportunity to watch the moon through the curtain of the falls. Arriving at a vantage point behind the falls, he was observing the moon when he was struck by a discharge of water and rock—the wind, which had been holding the falls away from the ledge, had ceased momentarily, and he was in the path of the falling water. He hung on, first to the ledge, later to a conveniently placed block of ice, until the water receded, then made a dash for safety.

The outline of events is the same for all three descriptions but the details are shifted to fit the requirements of each. In the journal entry, there is no expression of Muir's motivation for going behind the falls beyond, "I thought it would be a fine thing to get back of the down-rushing waters and see them in all their glory with the moonlight sifting through them." In the letter to Mrs. Carr his only explanation was that he supposed he was "in a trance." Motivation is left out entirely in the final form, since the fact that the ledge and view were there, as the mountain was to Hillary, was sufficient explanation.

The ledge (which is a ledge in the journal, a seam in the letter, and a "narrow bench" in *The Yosemite*) is not described in detail in any of the accounts, but in the journal Muir does state that at one point it was "only six inches wide." When he arrived at the proper location, he "was gazing up and out through the thin half-translucent edge of the fall" in the journal. In the letter he gazed "past the thin edge of the fall and away beneath the column to the brow of the rock." This element of the description is greatly expanded in *The Yosemite*:

> The effect was enchanting: fine savage music sounding above, beneath, around me; while the moon, apparently in the very midst of the rushing waters, seemed to be struggling to keep her place, on account of the ever-varying form and density of the water masses through which she was seen, now darkly veiled, or eclipsed by a rush of the thick-headed comets, now flashing out through openings between their tails. I was in fairyland between the dark wall and the wild throng of illumined waters.

In the journal Muir has some kind of warning about the sudden shift of the waters: "some heavy plashes striking the wall above me caught my attention." The same event is described in the letter, but there is no mention of it in the final form. The description of the sudden shifting of the water to batter Muir shows a progressive artificiality in Muir's effort to suggest not the event so much as its effect upon him. In the journal he wrote, "then suddenly all was dark." The letter to Mrs. Carr has, "suddenly I was darkened." *The Yosemite* version shifts to the comparative artificiality of a literary allusion: "like the witch-scene in Alloway Kirk, 'in an instant all was dark.'"

The pelting by the water and detritus of the falls is given in detail in the journal, but understated in the letter. "Down came a dash of outside gauze tissue made of spent comets, thin and harmless to look at a mile off, but desperately solid and stony when they strike one's shoulders. It seemed as if I was being pelted with a mixture of choking spray and gravel." This became in the letter, "down came a section of the outside tissue composed of spent comets." For the final version, Muir retained the spent comets and added, "thin and harmless looking in the distance, . . . they felt desperately solid and stony when they struck my shoulders, like a mixture of choking spray and gravel with big hailstones." The addition of the hailstones changes the picture considerably and is effectively allusive, since it recalls a situation that most readers have experienced, while the "choking spray and gravel" is certainly not in the common run of experience.

Muir's sensations of fear, his gripping and holding on to the ledge, and his final escape are the most changed elements in the anecdote. In the journal Muir "grasped an angle of the ledge and held hard with my knees." In the letter he "crouched low . . . and anchored to some angular flakes of rock." In the final version he dropped to his knees and "gripped an angle of the rock, curled up like a young fern frond with my face pressed against my breast." In the journal he "submitted to my frightful baptism with but little faith"; in the letter he "took my baptism with moderately good faith"; but in the final form, having sensed the inappropriateness of baptism as an image, Muir records that he "submitted as best I could to my thundering bath."

At that point in the final account only occurs an extended description of Muir's thoughts during his predicament, and it is prefaced by the comment, "how fast one's thoughts burn in such times of stress!" Also, when he is given a moment's respite from the pounding, he "pounced" to a position back of some ice in both early versions; but he "wedged" himself in the final account and "lay face downwards until the steadiness of the light gave encouragement to rise and get away." Both early accounts also give more details of his drying himself and preparing for sleep than the last account does.

The effect of all the changes is to make the final version of the anecdote the most readable. The extended detail of the view from behind the falls gives a more effective contrast to the events that follow. Heightened images, like the picture of

Muir "curled up like a young fern frond," make the situation more visual, while adding to the naturalness of the circumstances. Ferns *do* bend with the forces of nature, as Muir found that he must too. The substitution of "thundering bath" for "baptism" relieves a false ircny. To compare the situation with a baptism is to suggest that an introduction to nature in its wild forms is harsh and cruel, an idea which Muir everywhere argues against. And finally, the increased amount of introspection contributes to the suspense of the incident. All in all, Muir has taken an exciting, true incident and has made it more exciting, more suspenseful, and infinitely more vivid. Between 1871, when he wrote the first two accounts, and 1911, when he gave the incident its final form, he had become a professional.

One can find examples of the *mot juste*, the perfectly poetic and unchangeable passage, throughout Muir's writings, but his very earliest works are much cruder than his mature ones. A certain flippancy may be found in *A Thousand-Mile Walk to the Gulf* and in the earliest journals, which later disappeared. Muir poked fun at the scientific pretensions of his host in Munfordville, Kentucky, for example, by impertinently discounting his "long lessons concerning roots and herbs for every mortal ill" (*A Thousand-Mile Walk*, 253). He makes easy generalizations which are at the same time trite and flippant about characters met on the walk to the Gulf and during his first year in California: "He was about eighteen years of age, and had tried the work of shepherd because he thought it would be easy, but the sheep, finding little to eat, roamed over the hills and levels of their pasture at a discontented pace, and in most disorderly and widespread companies, making the limbs of the gentle shepherd weary in their pursuit" (*John of the Mountains*, 3). In time, Muir learned to withhold this kind of judgment unless he could produce evidence, in the form of action, to back it up.

His early writing also has a higher concentration of vague description. Idioms like "the unfielded plain," "wild and dismal nights," and the omnipresent "glorious" and "noble" applied to landscape are more common by far in the early journals than in the later works intended for publication. His later writings are more likely to reveal examples of sharp illuminating metaphors and adjectives, as in this description of a reindeer's antlers: "all are now in the velvet, some of which is beginning to peel off and hang in loose shreds about the heads of some of them, producing a very singular appearance, as if they had been fighting a rag-bag" (*Cruise of the Corwin*, 232).

It is worth noting, however, that Muir's writing does not improve in a constantly rising curve. Somewhat amateurish at the start of his career, his writing became somewhat stilted at its end. His middle years—the years of most of his periodical contributions, 1870 to 1890—mark his high point as a writer. During these years his imagery is most vibrant; his concepts of nature are most shocking, yet still effective and believable; and his sense of the right word, the perfect metaphor, the exact example is most striking. Before the journal which became *My First Summer in the Sierra*, Muir's thoughts on nature and life were still in the process of formation. After the writing of the periodical articles which make up *The Mountains of California*, his iconoclasm became somewhat tamed and reasonable. Neither the earlier nor the later situation was perfect for the kind of vigorous prose found in "Wild Wool," *My First Summer*, or *The Mountains of California*. The thorough professionalism of his last works help to overcome the loss of *elan* of his middle years, but the result is not quite up to the most powerful works of his most fertile period.

Norman Foerster has pointed out that Muir's prose is at its best when he is describing some kind of movement.[6] He is quite right, both because of the physical advantage movement gives the describer (allowing the use of a combination of descriptive and narrative techniques), and because Muir's feelings about nature are more attuned to flow and movement than to stillness. Descriptions of wind storms, floods, the earthquake in the Yosemite, or an iceberg's breaking off from the Muir Glacier are all more successfully realized than attempts at panorama from, for example, atop Mount Ritter.

Muir realized that static description could be deadening through dependence upon adjectives, and he worked hard to liven such descriptions. Some of his best efforts in this direction are drawn, by analogy, from his geological studies. His longest and most general description of the Sierra Nevada uses a metaphor of a bread slice, corresponding with the technical use of a geological cross-section:

> Were we to cross cut the Sierra Nevada into blocks a dozen miles or so in thickness, each section would contain a Yosemite Valley and a river, together with a bright array of lakes and meadows, rocks and forests. The grandeur and inexhaustible

beauty of each block would be so vast and over-satisfying that to choose among them would be like selecting slices of bread cut from the same loaf. One bread-slice might have burnt spots, answering to craters; another would be more browned; another, more crusted or raggedly cut; but all essentially the same. . . . Nevertheless, we all would choose the Merced slice, because, being easier of access, it has been nibbled and tasted and pronounced very good; and because of the concentrated form of its Yosemite, caused by certain conditions of baking, yeasting, and glacier-frosting of this portion of the great Sierra loaf.

(*A Thousand-Mile Walk,* 400)

I would not want to suggest that the metaphor is totally successful, exaggerated as it is in many of its particulars. It does, however, show Muir self-consciously working toward the use of natural metaphors of geology for static description. His use of the geological technique of foreshortening distance to describe landscape is a similar adaptation of the methods of geology to the purposes of prose. Describing the view from Glenora Peak in Alaska, Muir enlivens what would otherwise be a dead panorama by foreshortening the distance among the "ranks" of peaks in the Coastal Range, neglecting the distances between them as if he were constructing a relief map: "Everywhere the peaks seem comparatively slender and closely packed, as if Nature had here been trying to see how many noble well-dressed mountains could be crowded into one grand range" (*Travels in Alaska,* 116).[7]

Neither of these devices could be suitable to Muir's purposes very often. The first leads to an exaggerative prose style which, however appealing it was to him in his youth, did not adequately suggest the dignity he found in nature later in life. More and more, as he continued to write about his experiences in the wilderness, he came to depend upon thematic opposition as an adjunct to description, and it was in this use of contrasts that most of his finest writing took shape. In order to examine his use of this technique more fully, we must first consider his adaptation of the Emersonian doctrines.

III *The Last Disciple of Concord*

Attempting a definition of Trancendentalism is a tricky business. Hawthorne, in "The Celestial Railway," noted that it was a peculiar feature of "Giant Transcendentalism" that nobody had ever been able to describe his "form, his features, his substance, and his nature generally." Those who think they have reduced the world view of Transcendentalism to a definable substance ought to consider Eliza Cook's definition of that important element of it, the oversoul: "the spiritual cognoscence of psychological irrefragibility connected with concutient ademption of incoluminent spirituality and etherialized contention of susultory concretion."

Muir avoided the pit-falls of Eliza Cook's Transcendental vision by not occupying himself very much with *a priori* reasoning about the nature of the universe. His Transcendentalism is, on the contrary, experiential; and, when Muir raises an abstract point, it is almost always as a result of a consideration of concrete experience. That is not to say that he was not conditioned by extensive reading in Emerson, Thoreau, and the Romantic poets to an idealistic interpretation of experience, but that the conditioning process in his case seems less important than the events themselves. Exactly the same thing might be said of Thoreau, but even he was more adapted than Muir to respond in a "normal" Transcendental pattern to the experiences of nature. Muir is, in fact, something of a Transcendental heretic, though the statement seems a contradiction in terms. Emerson insisted that there was "no such thing as a Transcendental *party*," that the essence of Transcendentalism consisted in "seething brains" of "admirable radicals" and "unsocial worshippers," who were free to draw their own conclusions from their own observations of nature.[8] Still, Muir's interpretations of the data of nature are exotic enough to give pause to the modern reader whose knowledge of American Transcendentalism has been gained through a study of Emerson and Thoreau.

Muir became acquainted with the writings of Emerson through the wife of his friend and teacher at the University of Wisconsin, Dr. Ezra Slocum Carr. Emersonian phrasing and ideas loom large in Muir's writings throughout his life, but he seems to have grown to prefer Thoreau as he got older. When he journeyed in Alaska with Young, it was Young who carried a volume of Emerson along—Muir took one of Thoreau (*Alaska Days with John Muir*, 67). Moreover, Muir's comments in journals and published writings alike, especially when they are critical of human nature, seem to owe more to Thoreau than to Emerson, especially during his younger years. His most effective short piece of prose, "Wild

Wool," is distinctively Thoreauvian, with its puns, waspishness, and intensive personal observations. In sundry writings he also paralleled his own observations of natural subjects to Thoreau's observations in *Walden*. His anecdote about loons almost duplicates Thoreau's, then goes beyond it (*Boyhood and Youth*, 123-27). His insect studies remind one forcibly of Thoreau's black and red ants (*Boyhood and Youth*, 92-93; *My First Summer*, 43-47, 138-41, 169-70); and his description of fishing as a child is very similar to Thoreau's (*Boyhood and Youth*, 94-95).

The originality of his observations on human nature in his journals, along with the violence of his imagery, also suggest Thoreau. At one point in his journal, Muir himself recognized the affinity by citing Thoreau when his own style closely paralleled that of *Walden*: "The butter-and-milk habit has seized most people; bread without butter or coffee without milk is an awful calamity, as if everything before being put in our mouth must first be held under a cow. I know from long experience that all these things are unnecessary. One may take a little simple clean bread and have nothing to do on these fine excursions but enjoy oneself. *Vide* Thoreau. It seems ridiculous that a man, especially when in the midst of his best pleasures, should have to go beneath a cow like a calf three times a day— never weaned" (*John of the Mountains*, p. 97). Thoreau's discontent with the uses of civilization struck a more responsive chord in him than did Emerson's cold spirituality.

But Muir is indebted to both Emerson and Thoreau: to Emerson, for a conditioning toward idealism in his view of nature and for a part of his prose style; to Thoreau, for his example of wildness (however tame when compared to Muir himself) and waspish independence, and for parts of his prose style too, although Muir later outgrew that influence. These similarities and debts are striking, and plainly show that Muir may be considered a transcontinental disciple of the Concord doctrine. Far more striking are the many areas in which the "seething brain" of that "unsocial worshipper" of nature, John Muir, developed his own philosophy of nature, in many ways far transcending the laws laid down in the comparative civilization of Concord and even of Walden Pond.

The principal difference between Muir and the Concord Transcendentalists centers around their feelings about "commodity." Emerson included commodity as the first and lowest of the four uses of nature in aid of man. Thoreau, in "Where I

Lived and What I Lived For," makes a show at least of considering the hard, commercial facts of life. Muir, in all his writings, makes no mention of commodity except to scorn its existence and necessity. If it were not for his need for bread, he says, his entire life would have been spent in contemplation of the beauty of nature. Muir, quite opposed to both Emerson and Thoreau, found commodity in all its forms a necessary evil at best and a corrupting force at worst. Emerson assumes in *Nature* that commodity may serve good ends, that "a man is fed, not that he may be fed, but that he may work." Muir believed that man must be fed, but that he ought not to believe that the feeding of him is an obligation of nature. "Beasts, fire, water, stones and corn serve [man]," wrote Emerson, an idea which Muir detested and which he contradicted at every opportunity. "Why does water drown its lord? Why do so many minerals poison him? Why are so many plants and fishes deadly enemies? Why is the lord of creation subjected to the same laws of life as his subjects?" (*A Thousand-Mile Walk*, 356). Muir saw the domestication of animals as a part of the eating process ("Wild Wool"), and he had nothing but scorn for what he called "$$$ geology." Emerson was content to live most of his life in Concord; and, when he did tour the grand natural beauties of Yosemite, he followed the advice of his Eastern friends and did not lie in the open one night with John Muir. Therein lies the difference between the two men.

Most of Emerson's observations on nature are *a priori,* most of Muir's *a posteriori.* Emerson wrote without benefit of much scientific training; Muir was a botanist and a geologist until he transcended the limitations of those sciences. Emerson's sympathies were primarily cultural and ethical; Muir had almost no interest in culture and had only a rough-and-ready (however pure) ethic. Emerson wrote in the tradition of German philosophy; Muir observed and wrote at least in part in the tradition of Anglo-American science. One could read all of Emerson and never guess that Darwin had existed; scientific and philosophic acceptance of the process of natural selection is everywhere evident in Muir.

When Emerson wrote that "the axioms of physics translate the laws of ethics," he had not considered either the lilies, how they grow, or the rights of the rattlesnake coiled beneath them. Muir, on the other hand, would agree that natural laws translate ethical laws, but he would add that these same laws are warped by man in his anthropocentric insistence that he is the lord of creation. Man stands, in relation to nature, as the most intelligent, strongest, most adaptable creature. But, Muir would add, the laws of man's ethics, as they relate to commodity, are identical with the wolf's the alligator's or the scorpion's. Existence is the primary good. When man takes away the (wild) existence of another creature—by shooting a wild duck or by taming and breeding wild sheep—he cannot justify his action ethically except as an action which any wild creature would do himself for survival, if he could. It is man's double standard to which Muir objects, the pious exploitation of wild nature for whatever cause, with the excuse that nature was made to support man.

It may be argued that Emerson, in the poem "The Rhodora," for example, presses the same point; that, on being asked "Whence is the flower?" he replies that "Beauty is its own excuse for being." Muir answered the same question, about the twining lily: it was made for itself (*My First Summer*, 26). Emerson makes a poem of the emotion surrounding the statement:

> . . . if eyes were made for seeing
> Then Beauty is its own excuse for being:
> Why thou wert there, O rival of the rose!
> I never thought to ask, I never knew:
> But in my simple ignorance, suppose
> The self-same Power that brought me there brought you.

Muir would simply be annoyed with the questioner, and he would not, moreover, be satisfied with this answer. Beauty is not its own excuse for being—*being is*. And Emerson is making man appear more important than he really is.

Muir avoids most moral reflections based, by analogy, upon nature. He will contradict a natural reflection which seems to him to violate what he has observed of natural laws. He will not believe that the agave makes a "mighty effort" to flower and then dies, because he has never seen and does not believe that there is in nature "a mighty effort or the need of one" (*A Thousand-Mile Walk*, 378). But when he is observing a natural phenomenon that seems ideally suited for moral analogy to man, Muir is content to describe the beauty of the phenomenon itself and leave human morals out of the picture entirely. An example is his description of the dwarf pine (*pinus albicaulis*) of the Sierra. Imagine Thoreau beginning a description of a plant with the sentence, "Pines are commonly regarded as sky-loving trees that must necessarily aspire or die," and continuing to describe a pine that "creeps lowly," yet endures "bravely to a more advanced age than many of its lofty relatives" (*Mountains of California*, 236-37). Thoreau, and most nature writers of considerably less talent, could not resist the opportunity to "point the moral and adorn the tale" with an analogy to man. Muir instead simply describes the plant itself, but so beautifully and sympathetically that one is awed by his capacity to sense and communicate the feelings of an insentient plant. The moral which he has eschewed might have been striking temporarily, but the simpler, more intense description is, in the long run, far better writing.

I seem to be saying that Muir is a better writer and even a better philosopher of nature than either Thoreau or Emerson. I think it would be more nearly correct to say that he is a better *observer* of nature than either man. He knew far more about nature and her workings than Emerson, and he was much more interested in those workings for themselves alone than was Thoreau. He was, in fact, more of a Transcendentalist than either of the great Concord writers to whom he owed so much. Both Emerson and Thoreau, in their writings, were willing to compromise their ideals to some extent. Muir almost never did. Emerson had no doubt about the comparative importance of the soul and the body, yet he included commodity as one of the uses of nature. Thoreau admitted the necessity of commodity tacitly by including in *Walden* a full account of his expenses, and he even justified them rather shamefacedly. Muir never wrote about the making of money or the other uses of the body, although he was as successful in his ten years of fruit-farming as either of his Concord brethren at their commercial pursuits. No, in Muir we have for the first time in the history of Transcendentalism a total separation of the soul and the body, a "nirvana of corporeal passivity," as Young described Muir's double existence (*Alaska Days with John Muir*, 22). Muir has described the phenomenon in himself with words that show his heritage from Emerson and the mystic independence he acquired by himself in his beloved mountains:

> No sane man in the hands of nature can doubt the doubleness of his life. Soul and body receive separate nourishment and separate exercise, and speedily reach a stage of development wherein each is easily known apart from the other. Living artificially, we seldom see much of our real selves. Our torpid

souls are hopelessly entangled with our torpid bodies, and not only is there a confused mingling of our own souls with our own bodies, but we hardly possess a separate existence from our neighbors.

The life of a mountaineer seems to be particularly favorable to the development of soul-life, as well as limb-life, each receiving abundance of exercise and abundance of food.

(*John of the Mountains,* 77)

Muir's comprehension of the necessity for physical hardship to produce the sublime has an Oriental cast, a factor which the modern Zen beatniks seem to have recognized in him.[9] After exhausting himself physically with a hard climb, he was ready to absorb the beauties of the scenery revealed to him with his body totally passive, only his soul actively engaged. Like Thoreau, he undertook to "lessen the denominator" of his existence, thereby to achieve integrity. The climbing of mountains was ideally suited to his purpose. The Sierra were to Muir what Walden Pond was to Thoreau: "If you are acquainted with the principle, what do you care for a myriad instances and applications?" (*Walden,* 65). By climbing his mountains, Muir learned to achieve whenever he wanted a sensation of bodilessness and of the extension of his soul—a condition and situation somehow purer than the modern manifestation of the same thing that is gained through lysurgic acid or mescaline, but no less habit-forming. His mystic experiences (which he did not seem to recognize as such) became a part of his total existence and made prolonged life in the lowlands intolerable to him.

But the extremity of his sensations made their communication even more difficult, as I have shown in Chapter 4. Able to communicate the fullness of his experience only indirectly, he chose to write more often for more practical purposes. His experiences were intensely personal and defied communication, but the preservation of the beauties of nature was at once an easier and a more pressing problem. Muir wrote, as he said when he saw the tracks of a herd of sheep in the wilderness near Shadow Lake, to keep "the money changers out of the temple" (*Mountains of California,* 134). Nearly all of his writings have a primary didactic purpose, either to justify his own concepts of nature and the eternity of creation, as in the glacier articles, or to urge the preservation of the wilderness to retain the possibility of the peace of soul which he had found blessed. One must read between the lines in Muir, and in his journals not immediately intended for publication, to find the kind of purpose which may be seen almost anywhere in Emerson or Thoreau. It is, paradoxically, the extremity of his Transcendental beliefs that makes him appear in his writings less of a Transcendentalist than they.

IV Nature and Culture

In all of American literature since Emerson and Thoreau one theme has been predominant—the opposition of nature and culture. The *natural* impulses of protagonists ranging from the cosmic "I" in "Song of Myself," through Huckleberry Finn and Lambert Strethers, to Isaac McCaslin have been opposed by a cultural force. Comedy results from the assertion of the natural force; the domestic tragedy of "adjustment" results from the contrary. Muir's chief virtue as a writer, it seems to me, is that in his writings this opposition may be observed most clearly and nakedly. Two impulses work on him as a man and as a character in every one of his writings. Nature, totally accepted by him with no apologies for its red teeth and claws, beckons to him; culture holds him back.

He is the better subject for a test case because his writings are not culturally ameliorated as Emerson's and Thoreau's are. Muir never finds it necessary to compromise with nature. He looks the Darwinian revelations in the face and finds them good. He would not find nature the servant of man, as Emerson did; nor would he feel with Thoreau that it was "of the last importance" even to be present at the rising of the sun. Nature continues, interminable, impassive; and Muir believed that a similar passive acceptance of nature made the finest rule of life. Emerson found that art was insignificant in comparison with nature, that it was only "a little chipping, baking, patching, and washing." Muir would go farther. Man's effects upon nature, he suggests, are improperly differentiated as "art." Actually, they are, to a certain point, as natural as nature itself; for they represent one aspect of man's fight for survival, which is, of course, a natural act.

Man, in crowning himself lord of creation, has created an artificial distinction between the "human" and the "wild" and all that pertains to these two. It is a distinction which Muir did not believe existed in fact. It is man's duty, as it is the wolf's and the crayfish's, to provide for himself and to survive as a species. In the interest of that obligation, man has the right, just as he has the capacity, to transform his environment to better suit his needs. So far so good. But, man alone of all creatures, transforms his environment foolishly by slaughtering buffaloes for their tongues, ruining watersheds for the pasturage of his sheep, even killing off herds of caribou because of his religious beliefs.

Furthermore, Muir observed that he, and he assumed that other men, had a sense of beauty, an esthetic, or, in a word, a soul. While he does not press the point in his writings, he is aware of the possibility that other animals, plants, and even minerals, might be also so blessed. But man, unlike the flower which blooms, as it were, gratuitously, seems dedicated to the repression of this other part of himself; and, in the process of manipulating his environment for his own survival (not in itself an ignoble action, remember), he seems to have forgotten completely about this other aspect of life. The opposition of culture and nature is a man-made distinction. Culture stands in the eyes of the materialist for everything which contributes to the welfare of mankind, and nature is eternally opposed to these ends. Muir, prominently in "Wild Wool" and more subtly in thousands of scattered references throughout his work, climbs his mountain peak or glacier and screams defiantly at cultured man, "Not so!"

All of the American Transcendental writers believed that commodity was worshiped to a damaging extent in America. Emerson wrote that "Things are in the saddle,/and ride mankind"; Thoreau, that "to get his shoestrings, [the farmer] speculates in herds of cattle." Muir concurs, but goes much farther. All of culture was, to him, as its derivation suggests, a refinement of the basic process of eating, and to this process all the powers of the mind of man in America had been dedicated. The beauty of a work of art to Muir was almost a contradiction in terms. Wildness, or nature, produces the only true beauty, and man seems to be working to destroy all vestiges of this esthetic in the name of culture.

To stress this idea, Muir uses art and artifice along with more usual symbols of commodity as a force in opposition to the sublimity he finds in wild nature. Examples are legion, and I have already pointed out many of them. "Wild Wool" is the most explicit statement of the opposition of nature and culture. The incident of Muir's climbing Mount Ritter, opposed to the anecdote of the two artists in *The Mountains of California,* is perhaps the most subtle example. But it is hardly less subtle than the contrast of Nelson's search for skulls to Muir's for landscapes in *The Cruise of the Corwin.* There are hundreds of such anecdotes of opposition scattered through Muir's works. In *The Story of My Boyhood and Youth,* the death of Muir's dog "Watch" for killing chickens is opposed to the irony of man's own wholesale consumption of chickens, and it is then amplified by Muir's observations on the fate of the passenger pigeon (68-69).

Observing a grove of sequoia in *Our National Parks,* he also remarked a very sharp contrast: "seedlings, saplings, young and middle-aged trees are grouped promisingly around the old patriarchs betraying no sign of approach to extinction. On the contrary, they seem to be saying, 'Everything is to our mind and we mean to live forever.' But, sad to tell, a lumber company was building a large mill and flume nearby" (316). Or, one final example shows the range of Muir's use of this technique: the ironic contast in Shepherd Billy's "Independence Day oration," a catalogue of grievances against Mr. Delaney for not supplying enough food to the camp. His complaint, revealing his dependence upon lowland food, is further contrasted with Muir's own perfect freedom, simply and beautifully described: "Everything rejoicing. Not a single cell or crystal unvisited or forgotten" (*My First Summer,* 76). In all of the examples cited, Muir uses ironic contrast of cultural and natural conditions, bound together usually only by their position in the text. Rarely does he feel the need to editorialize, to point the moral, or even to point out the symbolism of his juxtapositions. The technique is inordinately subtle; so subtle, in fact, that as far as I know no critic has ever noted it. Yet it is the dominant technique in Muir's writing and the key to a real comprehension of his prose style. Like Thoreau, he is fundamentally an ironist; also like Thoreau, his irony is so fine that he has been misread for many years.

Muir had by heart and was fond of repeating the lines from Wordsworth,

> One impulse from a vernal wood
> Will teach you more of man,
> Of moral evil and of good,
> Than all the sages can.
> (*Alaska Days with John Muir,* 97)

Muir believed in that idea completely. His ethic and his esthetic were the same, and both were founded upon a complete identification with nature. What was natural must be good, what was artificial must be, however close to perfection, less good than its natural counterpart. His violent antipathy to the pastoralism of the "hoofed locusts" can be explained only by his feeling that the care of sheep *pretended* to a naturalism that it really did not have. In his eyes, this hypocrisy, furthered by art, was the worst sin of sheep herding. Muir made no "adjustment" to society and materialism, at least not in his writing. Like Thoreau, he was ever a gadfly to the domestic and domesticated virtues. Unlike Thoreau, he wrote no masterpiece to set forth his ideas in one artistic if commercially unpalatable dose. The result is that today he is esteemed more than he should be for reasons which are often inappropriate, and he is forgotten by the liberal and Romantic intellectuals who could profit most from him.

V *Critic of Life,* a fortiori

In his excellent chapter on John Muir in *Nature in American Literature,* Norman Foerster wrote that "one does not go to John Muir for a criticism of life. He understood neither the heights and depths of his own nature, which he avoided as most of us avoid the dizzy heights and depths of the material world, nor the complexities of social life—the boundless results of man's being a gregarious animal" (255). In a sense it is true that Muir did not even understand the complexities of many of the causes he espoused. His view on conservation was, to say the least, one-sided. Furthermore, if we are to consider adjustment to the complexities of society the foremost good of literature, Muir must be a damaging influence. His position is an extreme one. It seems, from his writing, that he abandoned his birthright of gregariousness to pursue a lonely course of absorption in nature. His example is, according to this view, like Thoreau's: it is inapplicable to the situation of common, garden-variety man.

Such observations are suggested by consideration of his work alone. Actually, Muir lived a full social life, including marriage, the making of money, and, as I have shown, a nagging loneliness which never totally deserted him, no matter how high the peak or how isolated the glacier. These incidents are hardly mentioned in his works. Why? Because they were to him the least important aspects of his life. The casual events of life, it must have seemed to him, were not proper material to be emphasized by inclusion within his works. In fact, throughout his writings there is much less emphasis on human processes than in the writings of any other naturalist, certainly less than in Thoreau. No one will ever learn to be a mountain climber by reading John Muir, while one easily perceives the mysteries of camping-out from *Walden*. Muir may describe the summit of Mount Shasta and the panorama visible from it in great detail, but he relates only casually the technique of his journey thither. Effects, processes of nature he fully describes, but his own actions, unless they are exceptional or contribute to the sublimity of the result, are left to the reader's imagination.

Part of the reason for his neglect of description of his own processes is a function of his difficulty with himself as auto-biographical hero, but much more important in his moral purpose in writing. Foerster says we must not go to Muir for a criticism of life. He is quite correct that we must not look in him for a criticism of the subtleties of life, but Muir's works do present an ideal of behavior and appreciation which mutely announces "go, thou, and do likewise." Whether aimed at the specific of preservation of natural beauty or as general inspiration to teeming masses to seek some solitude of wilderness for communion with nature, his writings are specifically moral and didactic. In this respect, he is again like Thoreau.

Foerster continued in his summary of Muir that, "when Emerson said of him that he was greater than Thoreau, he must have been thinking of Thoreau the naturalist. It is as a literary naturalist that Muir is perhaps greater than Thoreau and certainly equal to Burroughs" (p. 255). I think there can be little doubt that Muir was a better naturalist than Thoreau, but I do not believe that he was a better moralist. Thoreau, a better writer than Muir, urged his moral program in *Walden* with greater subtlety than Muir was capable of. Emerson's comment meant, however, that he found Muir's moral position more coherent, more considered, and more ideally suited to the life of the soul than Thoreau's.

Muir's morality was founded on a scientific knowledge considerably greater than Thoreau's. He embraced a comprehension of both botany and geology compared to which Thoreau's observations on the flora and geological structure of Walden Pond are quite elementary. But Muir's scientific knowledge was only a foundation for an extensive and intricate teleology. Like Thoreau and Emerson, he saw design everywhere. Unlike them, he did not believe that the evidence of creation was intended primarily for the sight of man alone. He believed, with Oriental religions, that man has the right, as every animal has, to partake of the perfections of creation, if he so wishes. Beyond that, his morality included not only the retention and preservation of this beauty from those who would destroy it in the name of commodity, but also his right and purpose to urge others to partake of it with himself.

One need not go to Muir for a criticism of life. Muir can be considered merely as a charming writer about nature. His books may, indeed, ought, to be read by anyone planning a tour of the Sierra Nevada, the Yosemite, or the coast of Alaska. But hidden beneath that apparently innocuous surface of description mingled with personal narration lies—like the nine-tenths of the icebergs which he described so well—a moral idealism that can puncture the materialistic assurance of an unsuspecting reader. It could cause him to reject his position at the bank, the broom factory, or the brokerage house in order to seek the sublimity of a mystic experience dawning upon him with the suddenness of a new moral law. We can grant Muir the finest accolade for a writer in modern society: his work can be "dangerous," for it does not pander to the accepted social norms.

Notes and References

Chapter One

1. Linnie Marsh Wolfe, *Son of the Wilderness; The Life of John Muir* (New York, 1945), p. ix.
2. Linnie Marsh Wolfe, ed., *John of the Mountains: The Unpublished Journals of John Muir* (Boston, 1938), pp. 102-3. Further references to this volume will be given in parenthesis in the text.
3. The Alaska travels are the only ones with any considerable literary interest, and are the only ones analyzed at any length in the present work.
4. Wolfe, *Son of the Wilderness*, p. 318.
5. John Muir, *The Cruise of the Corwin*, William Frederick Badé, ed., Volume VII of *The Sierra Edition of the Works of John Muir* (Boston, 1918), 36. All further references to Muir's writings, unless otherwise cited, are given in parenthesis in the text and refer to the volumes in The Sierra Edition.
6. Wolfe, *Son of the Wilderness*, p. 9.
7. Milton S. Griswold was a graduate in the Classics section of the University of Wisconsin, Class of 1862, and a friend of Muir's at the University (Wolfe, *Son of the Wilderness*, p. 80). I do not doubt his existence, but I do doubt that the incident took place in the manner Muir described.
8. Edith J. Hadley, "John Muir's Views of Nature and their Consequences," unpublished Ph. D. dissertation (Madison, Wisconsin, The University of Wisconsin, 1956), pp. 118-29, *passim*.

Chapter Two

1. Letter to Emily Pelton, January 29, 1870, Pelton Papers, Wisconsin State Historical Society, quoted in Wolfe, *Son of the Wilderness*, p. 63.
2. Undated letter to Mrs. Pelton, Pelton Papers, Wisconsin State Historical Society. Hereafter cited as "Pelton Papers."
3. Quoted in Badé, *Life and Letters of John Muir*, I, 67.
4. Pelton Papers; quoted in Badé, *Life and Letters*, I, 106.
5. Pelton Papers.
6. Included in an undated letter, Pelton Papers. The italics are Muir's.
7. *Walk*, pp. 361-62. This is only the first of many instances in

which Muir represents himself as at home in storms of various types. As will be seen, the representation of storms as a part of the orderly processes of nature becomes very important in his writing.

8. As I pointed out earlier in this chapter, Muir overcame a fantastic fear of these animals.

Chapter Three

1. *The Yosemite* (New York, 1912), p. 4.
2. Wolfe, *John of the Mountains,* pp. 2-8. References to this work and to "Twenty Hill Hollow," pages 400-16 in *A Thousand-Mile Walk to the Gulf* will hereafter be given in the text.
3. See Norman Foerster, *Nature in American Literature* (New York, 1958), p. 256. Foerster is quite correct in pointing out that Muir's best natural descriptions are those pointing out flux in what seems immovable, but Foerster does seem to suggest that such description is rather rare in Muir's writing. Rather, I believe it permeates *all* his writing except *The Story of my Boyhood and Youth.*
4. The chronology of Muir's writing is always difficult, for many volumes published late in his life use journal entries of a much earlier period. Although *The Mountains of California* was published before *My First Summer in the Sierra,* the observations recorded in this book preceded those of *The Mountains of California.*

Chapter Four

1. Quoted in Wolfe, *Son of the Wilderness,* p. 131.
2. Muir recognized the beauty of this image. He used it again, only very slightly changed, in *My First Summer in the Sierra,* p. 87: "We are camped for the night, our big fire, heaped high with rosiny logs and branches, is blazing like a sunrise, gladly giving back the light slowly sifted from the sunbeams of centuries of summers."
3. All of the articles which first appeared in *The Overland Monthly* have been gathered in *Studies of the Sierra,* William E. Colby, ed. (San Francisco, 1950). The citation here is from p. 32; other citations are given in parenthesis in the text.
4. Muir's account of the experience is given in *Our National Parks,* pp. 144-50. See also James B. Thayer, *A Western Journey with Mr. Emerson* (Boston, 1884).
5. Quoted in Wolfe, *Son of the Wilderness,* p. 190.
6. See *Mountains of California,* I, 47-54, *Steep Trails,* pp. 57-81.
7. The experience as described in *The Mountains of California* is most unlike what seems to have been the parallel real experience as given in Muir's journals. See *John of the Mountains,* pp. 147-50.
8. *Steep Trails,* v. "A Geologist's Winter Walk" was written in 1873, "Wild Wool" in 1875.

9. Robert Underwood Johnson, *Remembered Yesterdays* (Boston, 1923), p. 287.

10. *Ibid.*, pp. 287-88. I must digress here, since I lie awake some nights thinking of Muir's feelings when the bill was passed: the labor of ten years of his life, come to fruition so amazingly quickly through the efforts of one Eastern editor and his magazine. What mixed emotions Muir must have had! Fortunately he died before Johnson published his bizarre and naïve account of the origin of the scheme—or perhaps it was unfortunate that Muir was denied that final chuckle over the affair.

11. He was seventy-three years old when he was writing the book.

12. Wolfe, *Son of the Wilderness,* p. 284.

Chapter Five

1. Quoted in Samuel Hall Young, *Alaska Days with John Muir* (Fleming Revell, 1915), p. 203. Other citations from this text given in parenthesis in the text.

2. Certain physical problems of these writings ought also to be mentioned. *Travels in Alaska* was left unfinished at Muir's death, and doubtless would have been revised considerably had Muir lived longer. Much of *The Cruise of the Corwin* was written originally for publication as a series of letters in the San Francisco *Evening Bulletin.*

3. See George Wharton James, "John Muir: Geologist, Explorer, Naturalist," *The Craftsman,* VII (March, 1905), 637-67, esp. 665-67. James's account is inaccurate on most of the points agreed upon in Muir's and Young's versions of the incident, but is not, as Muir suggests in *Travels in Alaska,* p. 69, unfair to Young. This incident, by the way, is the only feat of heroism included in any of Muir's works; but it is not, according to Linnie Marsh Wolfe, the only time Muir ever saved someone's life. See *Son of the Wilderness,* p. 208.

4. Wolfe, *Son of the Wilderness,* p. 215.

5. *Ibid.*, p. 221; Young, *Alaska Days with John Muir,* p. 130.

6. *Cruise of the Corwin,* ix.

7. Muir never explains this most interesting phenomenon, although he does indirectly suggest the rational explanation I have given. This rational explanation might be supplemented with the psychological observation that such reactions as those exhibited by the Eskimos here are common, though hidden in the subconscious, to civilized human nature as well.

Chapter Six

1. Though examples are hardly needed, the Ahwahnee in Yosemite National Park included in their advertisement in *The New*

Notes and References

Yorker for July 13, 1963, the following: "Here, Nature slakes the spiritual thirst. As daily a refreshment as our teas at five."

2. I have been assured by Professor Hugh Iltis, curator of the botanical collection at the University of Wisconsin, that to the best of his knowledge Muir's botanical observations, at least, were not specific nor ordered enough to be more than minimally valuable, scientifically.

3. *Travels in Alaska*, p. 131.

4. Edwin Way Teale, *The Wilderness World of John Muir* (Boston, 1954), p. xv.

5. For the journal account, see *John of the Mountains*, pp. 61-62; the second account is in a letter to Mrs. Ezra S. Carr, quoted in Badé, *Life and Letters*, I, 249-52; the final account was in *The Yosemite*—see *The Mountains of California*, II, 163-65.

6. *Nature in American Literature* (New York, 1950), p. 258.

7. See also Thoreau, "The Pond in Winter," *Walden*, Riverside Ed., pp. 198-99, where he makes similar observations.

8. In "The Transcendentalist," *The Complete Essays and Other Writings* (Modern Library), pp. 92-94.

9. See, for example, Jack Kerouac, *The Dharma Bums*. I am unsure about how much of Muir's writing is really understood by Kerouac and others.

Selected Bibliography

PRIMARY SOURCES

The Mountains of California. New York, Century Company, 1894. Enlarged edition, 1911.

Our National Parks. Boston, Houghton Mifflin, 1901. Enlarged edition, 1909.

Stickeen. Boston, Houghton Mifflin, 1909.

My First Summer in the Sierra. Boston, Houghton Mifflin, 1911.

The Yosemite. New York, Century Company, 1912.

Edward Henry Harriman. New York, Doubleday Page, 1912.

The Story of My Boyhood and Youth. Boston, Houghton Mifflin, 1913.

Works; The Sierra Edition. William Frederick Badé, ed. Ten volumes. Boston, Houghton Mifflin, 1915-1924.

    I. *The Story of My Boyhood and Youth* and *A Thousand-Mile Walk to the Gulf.*

    II. *My First Summer in the Sierra.*

    III. *Travels in Alaska.*

    IV. & V. *The Mountains of California.*

    VI. *Our National Parks.*

    VII. *The Cruise of the Corwin.*

    VIII. *Steep Trails.*

    IX. & X. *Life and Letters,* by William F. Badé.

Studies in the Sierra. William E. Colby, ed. San Francisco, The Sierra Club, 1950.

John of the Mountains: The Unpublished Journals of John Muir. Linnie Marsh Wolfe, ed. Boston, Houghton Mifflin, 1938.

Picturesque California and the Regions West of the Rocky Mountains from Alaska to Mexico. San Francisco, Dewing and Co., 1888. [Edited by Muir, and includes six articles by him.]

Letters to a Friend. Jeanne C. Carr, ed. Boston, Houghton Mifflin, 1915. [Muir's letters to Mrs. Carr, 1866-1879.]

SECONDARY SOURCES

The following list includes only studies which have been mentioned in the text or are considered by the author to be generally useful. Much has been written about John Muir which is almost entirely biographical; the following list is restricted to works which have some critical merit.

FOERSTER, NORMAN. *Nature in American Literature.* New York, Russell and Russell, 1950. The section on Muir, pp. 238-63, though brief, is the most perceptive published analysis of Muir's position in the history of American Transcendental writing.

HADLEY, EDITH JANE. "John Muir's Views of Nature and Their Consequences." Unpublished Ph.D. dissertation, Madison, Wisconsin, University of Wisconsin, 1956. An exceedingly thorough study of Muir, both biographically and critically. Unfortunately, the writing is somewhat discursive.

JAMES, GEORGE WHARTON. "John Muir: Geologist, Explorer, Naturalist." *The Craftsman,* VII (March, 1905), 637-67. See above, Note 3, Chapter V. The essay is unfortunately typical of much of the writing about Muir published during his lifetime.

JOHNSON, ROBERT UNDERWOOD. *Remembered Yesterdays.* Boston, Little Brown, 1923. Pages 278-316 treat Muir's and Johnson's activities in the national parks movement.

MERRIAM, C. HART, ed. *The Harriman Alaska Expedition.* Fourteen volumes. New York, Doubleday, 1901. The mountain labored and gave birth to another mountain.

TEALE, EDWIN WAY, ed. *The Wilderness World of John Muir.* Boston, Houghton Mifflin, 1954. Though this volume is an anthology of selections from Muir's writings, the selections have been edited and introduced with enough comment that it seems best to list it among secondary works. As an anthology, it has been selected to illustrate Muir's life more than to suggest his greatness as a writer.

THAYER, JAMES BRADLEY. *A Western Journey with Mr. Emerson.* Boston, Little Brown, 1884. See above, Note 4, Chapter IV.

WOLFE, LINNIE MARSH. *Son of the Wilderness; the Life of John Muir.* New York, Knopf, 1945. An almost entirely uncritical biography. Well researched into the details of Muir's life, the book makes almost no attempt to analyze Muir's position as a writer or as a thinker.

YOUNG, SAMUEL HALL. *Alaska Days with John Muir.* New York, Fleming Revell, 1915. A delightful reminiscence; well-written; extremely valuable to the student of Muir (see above, Chapter V.)

Index

Index